PIRANESI AT THE AGE OF THIRTY

GIOVANNI BATTISTA PIRANESI

BY

A. HYATT MAYOR

H. BITTNER AND COMPANY, PUBLISHERS · NEW YORK
1952

This book was printed for H. Bittner and Company, Publishers, in New York City. Text: The Anthoensen Press. Plates: The Meriden Gravure Company. Binding: Russell-Rutter Company, Inc. Book Design: Herbert Bittner.

For

JÁNOS SCHOLZ

from

the Author

and

the Publisher

AN APPRECIATION

This book would lack some of its most important elements had it not been for the kindness of Mr. Frederick B. Adams, Jr., and Miss Felice Staempfle of the Morgan Library in doing everything to make available the treasures of Piranesi drawings in their care.

The greatest thanks are also due to Mr. Philip Hofer, Mr. János Scholz and Mr. Walter Schatzki for generously allowing the reproduction of their drawings.

The first inspiration for the book, and the continuing care, encouragement, correction and suggestion have all come from Mr. Herbert Bittner.

TABLE OF CONTENTS

LIFE

IT IS A LITTLE DISCOURAGING TO WRITE ABOUT PIRANESI BEcause there once existed two accounts of his life which, if they ever come to light, will supersede much that has been printed about him. The most important of these accounts is his autobiography which was written on "a bundle of many pages." A year after his death his first biographer mentioned this bundle and aggravates our regret at its disappearance by saying that Piranesi's life, if all could be told, would make a book as tumultuous as Cellini's.

The second account was a life written by Piranesi's sons from their father's autobiography and from their own recollection. In 1798 the sons took this manuscript to Paris where a Frenchman drew on it for a biography that still exists in manuscript at the Bibliothèque Nationale. By the late 1820's the sons' manuscript had come to a London publisher who flirted with the idea of printing it. Nothing came of this project but a partial paraphrase in *The Library of the Fine Arts* for August, 1831. The autobiography may well be lost, but the sons' manuscript could turn up tomorrow in some English country house or on a back shelf in the Bodleian Library.

The sources that remain tell little about Piranesi's youth and almost nothing about his ancestors. His family might have come from the town of Pirano in Istria since he often wrote his name in the adjectival form of Piranese. Giovanni Battista was born on October 4, 1720, at a village called Mojano or Mogliano near Mestre and was christened a month and four days later at Venice, about ten miles away. Since parents rarely waited so long to baptize a baby, his father, Angelo Piranese, may have been taken out of his home parish by his work as a stone mason. His mother, Laura Lucchesi, was the sister of Matteo Lucchesi, a civil engineer and architect who is said to have been the boy's first instructor in the art of building. This uncle Matteo worked in one of the most important departments of the Venetian state, the Magistrato delle Acque, that had charge of harbor constructions. In the last years of the Republic, Venice built few new houses or churches but was constantly repairing and constructing docks, bridges and sea walls. Just a little before the last doge abdicated Venice carried through one of the greatest public works in

1

all its history—the miles of sea walls and cyclopean riprap that prevent the Adriatic from washing through the harbor barrier of sand bars. Almost anywhere one could hear some gang of men pulling up the weight of a pile driver and singing work songs to the pile as they pounded it down to the tremendous caverns of the sea:

A basso a fondi
A fondi del mare
E va a ritrovare
I suoi compagni
Delle caverne
Orrende scure
Delle caverne
Orrende grotte.

The coffer dams being sucked dry by the pumps, the piles being rammed down deep under the level of the tides, the foundation stones being lowered from scows to the exposed mud of the lagoon—all these sights and sounds that dwarf the men who make them, these must have been among Giovanni Battista Piranesi's earliest boyhood memories. And when the day's work was done he must have heard more about great projects from his father, the stone mason, and his uncle, the engineer. Thanks to this boyhood background, Piranesi as a grown man in Rome was always to imagine how the huge, ruined halls and aqueducts must have looked when they were being assembled on their foundations, what tackle and scaffolding must have served to raise their arches so durably aloft.

This uncle, the engineer and architect, is worth a word or two, for his character sounds so like Piranesi's that he must have helped to shape his nephew's mind. Matteo Lucchesi was not a modern specialist with a slide rule. He was an eighteenth-century Venetian, which means an individualist restless with curiosity, inquiring into all kinds of things, prompt to argue any intellectual point, and forever trying to create despite Italy's poverty and political stagnation. When he was twenty-five, and his nephew ten, he brashly attacked an historical discovery advanced by Scipione Maffei, the dramatist and archaeologist who then led intellectual circles in northern Italy. Lucchesi's pamphlet *On the Pretended Discovery of a Tuscan Entablature* is interesting because in it he mentions a theory of the Etruscan origin of Greek art that his nephew was to defend for years with ink and energy. He went back a century and a half to the architect Scamozzi for his authority in claiming that the Doric order of columns and entablature was really invented by the Tus-

2

cans, or Etruscans, and was then taken over and named by their Greek conquerors the Dorians. The Italic origin of Greek art became the faith by which Piranesi was to live and die.

Lucchesi also gave his nephew his veneration for architecture. "Architecture," he wrote, "which is now in deeper eclipse than any other art, directs works that approach the idea of Creation." He constructed a bridge and a palace with a fine stair on the mainland, but in the city of Venice itself his only architectural commissions were to remodel a couple of old buildings. He rebuilt the Church of St. John in Oil on the pattern of Palladio's beautiful church of the Redeemer. Palladio's interior, always unfolding in a mystery of light and space, seems not to have satisfied Lucchesi, for he called his "improved" imitation The Redeemer Redeemed. Uncle and nephew are said to have quarrelled. They were so much alike that they could not but fall out.

Piranesi's region produced almost all the great Italian architects since Michelangelo. The long tradition of northern Italy strengthened his family background and fixed his ambition to become an architect. Many years later, long after he must have abandoned all hope of designing great buildings, he still persistently signed himself ARCHITETTO VENEZIANO. He prepared himself for his career by studying with various masters, but probably quarrelled with them as he had with his uncle Matteo. It is final to quarrel with a teacher, for after you have slammed the door it is hard to go back the next day, but it is less drastic to lose your temper with a book, for it will stay in the corner where you threw it until you cool off and resume your studies.

Piranesi is said to have taken lessons from Ferdinando Bibiena, then old and blind in Bologna, but much more probably studied his handbook *L'Architettura Civile,* first published in 1711. The number of inexpensive pocket editions show that this manual became required reading for Italian architectural students. This it deserved to do, for it summed up what an architect had to know about geometry and calculation, building methods and materials, house planning, handy detail for doors and windows, the five orders of columns and entablatures, perspective for renderings and stage sets, and construction machinery. The chapters on perspective contained some diagrams and pictures that started all stage decorators drawing buildings at an angle, with walls fleeing away right and left into the distance. This diagonal scheme reappears throughout Piranesi's work (fig. 6). Bibiena does not write much about the perspective of circular buildings, which Piranesi often miscalculated.

The Morgan Library has two sheets of sketches that Mr. Willard C. Clifford has identified as copies from Johann Bernhard Fischer von Erlach's *Entwurff einer his-*

3

torischen Architectur, first printed in Vienna one year after Piranesi was born. This Project for a History of Architecture was the first—and for many years the only—comprehensive picture book of famous ancient and oriental buildings. The illustrations range as far afield as Siam, China, Spalato, Palmyra and Stonehenge. Where Fischer could get accurate pictures he made the buildings recognizable. Egypt and Greece were still so untravelled that Fischer's fanciful pictures of Pyramids or his meagre diagram that misrepresents the Parthenon are more fantastic than his comparatively truthful engraving of the remote Persian cliff carvings. Piranesi must have heard of many of these faraway wonders from the sailor friends of his maternal grandfather, who was a sea captain. Fischer's strange book would have meant more to a Venetian, at the crossroads of the world, than to an inland Roman or Florentine. Piranesi must have admired the book for a number of reasons—for its glimpses of the exotic, for the encyclopaedic sweep of its erudition, and for the grandeur of its imaginary reconstruction of halls tower high and walls to the horizon.

Piranesi, like all his Italian contemporaries, formed his taste on Palladio's *Architettura*, which had less influence when it was first published in 1570, than in the eighteenth century when it came to dominate Italian, English and American practice. Palladio's illustrations familiarized Piranesi with Roman buildings long before he went to Rome. His human harmony, and some of his actual architectural schemes appear in Piranesi's first designs. After years in Rome Palladio's clarity and elegance gave way to Piranesi's own baroque sombreness and conflict.

Although the Venice in which Piranesi grew up had no room or cash for new buildings in brick and stone, it did give scope for the tinsel perspectives of the stage. The many opera houses in that pleasure resort did not attract their international audiences by well-written plays, but by the ingenious contrivance of their scenery. The floors of their stages sloped up to backdrops painted with endless flights of balustraded stairs and domes beyond domes. Since the glimmering of the candles killed most color and revealed only lines and masses, the illusion of immensity depended on the adroit rendering of light and shade and a mastery of the mathematics of perspective. All Italian stage designers once possessed a synthesis of skills that would be hard to equal in a scenery studio today. By going to school at this exacting craft, Piranesi learned to focus light and shade with dramatic effect, to draw buildings from the most imposing angle, to sketch with accurate boldness, and to dare any stunt in perspective.

But when the masquerade of eighteenth-century Venice jarred on his longings for grandeur, he fled to an elder brother, a monk, who read to him from ancient his-

4

tory and fired him with a determination to know Rome. He must have heard still more about ancient Rome from his uncle Matteo, who wrote good Latin and had studied all the main Italian and French books on architecture. Rome became the center of his world—Roma caput mundi—the only place, as Poussin said, where great works could be conceived. This vision was to direct his life and was to survive even the attrition of many years of familiarity with the actual city. But his poverty and his meagre education outside his art seemed to promise slight chances of reaching Rome until, when he was twenty, he had the luck to be taken as a draughtsman on the staff of a new Venetian ambassador to the Vatican.

Rome opened one world to him even as it closed another. He had hoped to rival the imperial ruins by designing as vastly and as boldly, but after being there for three years he wrote "no buildings of today display the magnificence of the old, such as the Forum of Nerva, the Colosseum or the Palace of Nero—nor is there a prince or private man inclined to create any such." The fact was that Church revenues had dwindled, and the Roman nobles could just afford to maintain their estates and their palaces without yet being forced, like their descendants, to refresh their fortunes by marrying foreign money. Piranesi met this check to his ambitions like a true Venetian. "I have no recourse except to follow other modern architects and make my ideas known through pictures." He therefore learned the typically Venetian art of etching and when he was twenty-three, published twelve large copper plates of projects for antique palaces, town squares, temples, etc., designed in the Palladian taste and on Fischer von Erlach's colossal scale. He also adapted actual details: from Palladio a rotunda of columns topped by a festooned architrave supporting statues (fig. 1), from Fischer one of the Karlskirche pillars, and a certain chubbiness in a sphinx. He hopefully called his first effort *The First Part of Architecture and Perspective.*

For two centuries lavishly illustrated books on architecture had been a specialty of northern Italy and particularly of Venice. Most of the great early editions of Vitruvius appeared there, and north Italian architects often printed designs that they had not been able to execute. Palladio's books show many villas as he would like to have built them if the money had not run out, or the patron had not changed his mind. The Romans ridiculed this north Italian itch to publish, for Rome, like Washington, is essentially a sterile place that imports creators because it cannot grow them at home. So poor young Piranesi's *First Part of Architecture* fell too flat to leave him any hope of ever achieving a second part. He had probably financed it with money from a builder called Nicola Giobbe who had lent him books, drawings and prints, had taken him into private collections, and introduced him to lead-

5

ing architects. In gratitude for this help the young man quite properly dedicated the resulting work to Giobbe.

After the failure of his first publication left him without funds, his father made matters desperate by stopping his starveling allowance of about $7.50 a month. Hunger then drove him home to Venice. There he may have painted scenery and is said to have worked in Tiepolo's studio. Tiepolo's style shows unmistakably in the four big etchings of *Grotesques* that he probably made at this time (figs. 4, 5). The open texture of the shadows and the ragged sparkle of the line come straight out of Tiepolo's etched *Caprices*.

From a distance Piranesi's *Grotesques* seem poised in brilliance like the sun god on the gilded gondola that he created for a carnival regatta (fig. 2) and they seem to flutter as flippantly as the cartouches that he designed for Venetian salons (fig. 3). But look closer. Instead of the expected cupids and ribbons, the charming jumble really consists of crumbling columns, asps under shattered coffins and skulls stuck with scraps of scalp. The light language of rococo Venice tells of nothing but ruin. Piranesi was not inventing a new mode. For two centuries north Italian artists had been fascinated with decay. Only he expressed it exuberantly.

It was probably during his short return to Venice that he achieved his first great artistic success, which was to affect stage sets throughout Europe and may have shaped Dance's design for Newgate Prison in London. This is the undated set of fourteen large etchings of *Imaginary Prisons* (figs. 9-23). Piranesi seems to have developed his idea for the *Prisons* out of a small project for opera scenery that Daniel Marot etched in 1702. Piranesi's first step was to enlarge and elaborate Marot's *Prison d'Amadis* into a *Dark Prison* that he published in his *First Part of Architecture*. The *Dark Prison* would count among Piranesi's good early etchings if he had not so far surpassed it later in his set of *Imaginary Prisons*. The *Prisons* are the romantic masterpiece of Piranesi's mid-twenties and as imaginative suggestion they are the masterpiece of his whole life. Only a stage-struck engineer could have conjured up these endless aisles, these beams draped with tons of chain, these gangplanks teetering from arch to arch, these piers that stand like beacons for exploring loftiness and light. No other prints involve the eye so deeply inward and upward. Piranesi rendered such more-than-Roman immensities like a true Venetian by letting his etching needle scribble and zigzag until it sketched areas of shade as translucent as a Guardi wash.

The *Prisons* show their origins in baroque opera sets by the intricacy of their perspective, the thrust and counter-thrust of their architectural masses, their diagonal axes with vanishing points right and left, and their Venetian passion for grandeur. Now that photography has robbed Piranesi's *Roman Views* of some of their former value as records, the *Prisons* stand out as one of his supreme achievements. They did not seem so to Piranesi's contemporaries, nor perhaps to Piranesi himself, for about fifteen years later he thoroughly re-etched the plates, adding archaeological ornaments, blackening shadows, defining structure more sharply and depth more solidly (figs. 13, 14). He had spent the interval between the first etching and the revision in drawing existing buildings until his early painterly lightness had changed to startling density, his suggestion into statement.

The *Prisons* anticipated the literature of romanticism, and the first description of them makes a famous page of English prose. In 1818 De Quincey wrote in his *Confessions of an English Opium Eater:*

"Many years ago, when I was looking over Piranesi's Antiquities of Rome, Mr. Coleridge, who was standing by, described to me a set of plates by that artist, called his Dreams, and which record the scenery of his own visions during the delirium of a fever. Some of them (I describe only from memory of Mr. Coleridge's account) represented vast gothic halls; on the floor of which stood all sorts of engines and machinery, wheels, cables, pulleys, levers, catapults, &c., &c., expressive of enormous power put forth, and resistance overcome. Creeping along the sides of the walls, you perceived a staircase; and upon it, groping his way upwards, was Piranesi himself; follow the stairs a little further, and you perceive it come to a sudden abrupt termination, without any balustrade, and allowing no step onwards to him who had reached the extremity except into the depths below. Whatever is to become of poor Piranesi, you suppose, at least, that his labours must in some way terminate here. But raise your eyes; and behold a second flight of stairs still higher; on which again Piranesi is perceived, by this time standing on the very brink of the abyss. Again elevate your eye, and a still more aerial flight of stairs is beheld; and again is poor Piranesi busy on his aspiring labours; and so on until the unfinished stairs and Piranesi both are lost in the upper gloom of the hall."

However inexact in detail, this hits the mood of the *Prisons*.

Coleridge must have been profoundly moved to utter a rhapsody that De Quincey could remember for years without ever having seen the pictures that had been described to him. De Quincey's vividness has made it impossible to describe the *Prisons* in English without paraphrasing him. Consciously or unconsciously, Melville did so in *Clarel* when he versified the *Opium Eater* in a kind of homemade *Xanadu,* and Aldous Huxley has shown more expertness in prose.

After a couple of years in Venice Piranesi again escaped—this time for good—by taking a consignment of Venetian prints to sell as the publisher's agent in Rome. There he set up shop in the middle of town on the Corso across the street from the French Academy, which was then in the Palazzo Salviati. He disposed of his Venetian prints so profitably that he could at last plan to settle permanently in his chosen city. The next thirty-three years were to make him the most famous Roman of his century. In antiquity nobody could really become a Roman. You had to be born. But ever since the Papacy reshaped the city, a celibate society, incapable of reproducing itself, has devised ways of absorbing outsiders quickly and completely. Since St. Peter, Rome has imported almost all her historians, artists and popes. Arriving one by one as mature men without marriage ties, the newcomers develop a social climber's curiosity in each local antiquity and parish custom, and die passionately wedded to Rome's traditions.

When Piranesi first settled there he did not know just where to begin. He was twenty-five. He did not care to design stage scenery, could not find work as an architect, and had failed as an architectural author. What was he to turn to next? Rome herself commanded him. As he wrote a few years later "When I saw in Rome how most of the remains of ancient buildings lay scattered through gardens and ploughed fields where they dwindled day by day, either weathering away, or being quarried into to steal fragments for new buildings, I resolved to preserve them by means of engravings. I have therefore drawn these ruins with all possible exquisiteness." He started modestly by etching little views of Rome that appeared later in a couple of guidebooks. His concentration enabled him to etch a plate a day for about $2.50 per etching. Meagre as these etchings look beside his mature work, their painterly quality puts them above the other illustrations with which they were published.

When he was twenty-eight he etched twenty-eight small views of *Roman Antiquities of the Age of the Republic* (figs. 7, 8) that are better known under the title that he gave them at their second issue: *Some Views of Triumphal Arches and other Monuments* (figs. 7, 8). They show that he had travelled with his sketchbook to Pola, Ancona, Verona, Rimini and Spoleto and could already capture freshness of air and spaces of light on little pages. But daintiness was not Piranesi's ambition. He wanted elbow room to draw on a grand scale, to stock up huge plates of copper and to publish monumental folios on the stoutest paper. But where was he to find the capital?

When he was thirty-two romance unexpectedly opened the way. His first biographer probably repeats an often told story when he says that Piranesi "was in the Forum one day drawing some of the venerable ruins when the daughter of a gardener passed by him with her sprightly little sister. 'Is she to be had in marriage?' asked Piranesi frankly. When the little girl as frankly answered yes, the young draughtsman cast down has paper and crayon, and then and there among the trees and cattle, after the fashion of the golden age, settled on this singular marriage."

The story appears in a truer context in the anonymous English paraphrase of the sons' life printed in *The Library of the Fine Arts,* 1831. This story is worth quoting at length, even though it comes to us at third hand, for it is the only personal anecdote that retains some of the suddenness and singularity that Piranesi must have put into his lost autobiography.

"He happened one Sunday to see the daughter of the gardener to the Prince Corsini, whose features, and especially her black eyes, perfectly convinced him that she was possessed of genuine descent from the ancient Romans; nor was her dowry of a hundred and fifty piastres (about $175) of small consideration in the scale, though the jealous watchfulness he maintained, was not entered into with merely mercenary motives. To his friends however he mentioned his intentions of marrying, because it would enable him to procure the means of beginning his work on Roman Antiquities; and the whole history of his courtship, as it appears to have been given in an account by himself, must be considered equally characteristic and amusing.

At the very first interview he asked her hand in marriage; and though his ardour frightened her at first, he contrived to obtain the consent of all parties to the celebration of their nuptials within five days afterwards. After the ceremony, he placed beside her dowry his finished plates and his unfinished designs, observing that their whole fortune was before her, but that in three years her portion should be doubled. He continued his labours and kept his word. They went to reside in the house now occupied by the celebrated Thorwaldsen, and seem to have lived on the whole happily, though his notions of the rights of a husband and father, founded on those of the *pater-familias* of the Romans, were no doubt carried to the extreme. In his ardent attention to his studies, his son complains that he would frequently forget his meals, in which case his young children, who did not dare to interrupt him, were often deprived of that nourishment which their tender age demanded."

Piranesi at once went full blast at a project that he had already started, and that became his biggest single undertaking. He first secured all available aid for the long pull ahead. The Pope allowed him to import two hundred bales of paper without paying customs duty. He obtained a promise of patronage from Lord Charlemont, a young Irishman who had set forth when he was eighteen to travel in Egypt and the Levant, and then in Rome was planning to set up a school for British artists like the long-established French Academy. Piranesi proposed to dedicate to Lord Charlemont a folio volume to be called *Ancient Sepulchral Monuments*. But as Piranesi worked on the project for five years, it grew into four folio volumes of over two hundred plates. After exhausting the tombs he investigated the bridges, theatres, aqueducts and other monuments of Rome. As he outgrew the first project he broadened the title to *Roman Antiquities*.

After two hundred years, the work still remains the vastest picture book of buildings and antiquities in Rome. Almost half of the plates record things that have since vanished or been further damaged. It is the first book that attempted to reassemble objects that had been found together and then scattered. The big plate of the Roman water system was the first painstaking reconstruction of far flung and complicated ruins, and alone cost him six months of drawing, digging and measuring. This book also went farther than previous attempts to interpret ancient remains in the light of ancient texts, and especially in the light of Vitruvius' description of Roman engineering practice. Renaissance architects had looked at ancient ruins with Vitruvius in hand in a way that Matteo Lucchesi must have taught Piranesi, but they had not used Vitruvius so thoroughly or gone to him for help in guessing at the foundations underground. Piranesi's method was right, even though he sometimes pictured Roman foundations as though they had been built by the modern engineering methods that he had learned in Venice.

Little as we know about Piranesi's teachers in art, we know less about his teachers in archaeology. As a boy his brother, the monk, had started him on Latin, and his uncle Matteo must have shown him all the main books on classical architecture. During his busy years in Rome antiquarian priests must have helped him with their classical learning, and are said to have written some of his prefaces for him. But his originality as an archaeologist lay in inspecting the Roman ruins through the eyes of his uncle the engineer. Discoveries are apt to occur when the training of one profession is diverted onto another. The intellectual curiosities of Rome in the 1750's and '60's show in the fact that Piranesi was suggesting some of the fundamental methods of modern archaeological excavation even while his adversary Winckelmann was inspiring classical archaeology with an emotional outlook.

The *Roman Antiquities* made a European sensation. France was already expecting the book, thanks to Piranesi's close connection with his neighbors in the French Academy and to the prospectus that his French publishers in Rome sent to important Parisians. Paris alone ordered two hundred copies, and Piranesi wrote a year later that he had sold two thousand to Germany, Denmark, Sweden and Russia, where they obtained a substantial patronage for him and his sons. Some nine months after the publication the Society of Antiquaries in London made an honorary member of "Il Signor Giovanni Battista Piranesi, a Venetian, resident in Rome, a most ingenious Architect, and author of the Antiquities of Rome and the Neighborhood." Recognition lagged behind at home, for he had to wait four years to be accepted into the local guild of painters, and eleven years to be created a *Cavaliere*. But for Europe in general the *Roman Antiquities* made Piranesi into a celebrity that every cultivated traveller considered as well worth having seen as the Colosseum.

Rarely has a private man accomplished so great a project with so little help. Outside the windfall of his wife's dowry, he received no aid beyond the remittance of customs duties on paper, for Lord Charlemont's promised patronage came to nothing, largely through the ill offices of the English agent who handled his affairs in Rome. The young Irishman who was twenty-eight when the *Roman Antiquities* was published, had already been governing Armagh for two years, and was taking advantage of the sessions of the House of Lords to throw himself into the London whirl of the Society of the *Dillettanti*. He was active and agreeable, but Dr. Johnson said of him "what did Lord Charlemont learn in all his travels, except that there was a snake in one of the pyramids of Egypt?"

But poor Piranesi had counted so heavily on Lord Charlemont's help that a year after the publication of the *Roman Antiquities* he circulated a pamphlet called *Letters of Justification written to Lord Charlemont and to his Agents in Rome*. He illustrated the booklet with reduced copies of the dedication pages that he had etched for the volumes of the *Roman Antiquities*. Wherever the big plates displayed his patron's name or coat of arms as though it were carved on an ancient monument, the little copies showed a cavity as though the honors had been gouged from the marble.

Only two years before, Dr. Johnson had composed his famous letter to Lord Chesterfield after completing his *Dictionary* unaided. Dr. Johnson might have been writing for Piranesi when he said "Seven years, my Lord, have now past, since I waited in your outward rooms, or was repulsed from your door; during which time I have been pushing on my work through difficulties, of which it is useless to complain, and have brought it, at last, to the verge of publication, without one act of assistance, one word of encouragement, or one smile of favour. Such treatment I did not expect, for I never had a patron before."

Piranesi was not more angry, but he spoke out in Latin boldness: "A nobleman must consider his ancestors, and an artist his descendants. A nobleman is the latest of his name, and an artist the first of his. Both must act with equal delicacy. . . . From now on I recognize no judge of my work except the public." He signed himself with his proud new title as Fellow of the Society of Antiquaries in London. The time had come when a man of genius could hope to make an independent living. Once intellectuals began to dispense with the protection of the nobility, the French Revolution could not be far off.

Piranesi's thirties were his years of truculence. As soon as he had published the *Roman Antiquities,* and even while he was rebuking Lord Charlemont, he started a gigantic polemical work called *The Magnificence and Architecture of the Romans.* He was angered by two attacks on ancient Rome from London and Paris. In 1755 a silly anonymous article in a London newspaper called the Romans "a gang of mere plunderers sprung from them who had been, but a little while before their conquest of Greece, naked thieves and runaway slaves." Then in 1758, after Piranesi had prepared to answer this article, the real threat came from another quarter when David Leroy published the first book ever devoted to Greek architecture, *Les Ruines des plus beaux Monuments de la Grèce.* Leroy claimed that the Greeks had invented an architecture which the Romans had then adapted. It astonishes us today to find that such an opinion ever caused astonishment. Europe knew Roman architecture well, but had no idea of the Greek, for few cultivated Europeans had penetrated the iron curtain of brigands and suspicious Turkish officials who made a visit to Greek ruins next to impossible.

On the other hand, Rome had dominated the West for over two thousand years until Romans, and indeed all Italians, had come to feel that nothing could have originated anywhere else. Not only Piranesi's uncle Matteo, but all his Italian contemporaries believed that the Etruscans, an older and more intelligent race than the Greeks, had handed on their inventions to the Romans. After the Romans conquered Greece, the Greeks had picked up a whimsical facility from the pioneer labors of ancient Italy. When Piranesi was a boy certain Frenchmen and Englishmen began to suspect that the Greeks had invented more art than the Italians allowed. The French and English attacks that roused Piranesi were just the beginning of one of the great revaluations of modern time. This revaluation struck with force in 1764 when Winckelmann's *History of Ancient Art* announced the vision (later a dogma) of the Greeks as Arcadians dwelling in ideal beauty and noble calm. Winckelmann allowed merit to Piranesi's etchings but naturally spurned his theories. In the narrow intellectual circles of the eighteenth-century Rome the two men, who were almost of the same age, avoided each other for thirteen years like wrestlers too wary to grapple—one the lofty rhapsodist of Greece, the other the heavyweight champion of Rome. Today both theorists seem equally arbitrary.

When Piranesi saw the threat to his faith he threw everything into the defense. After five years of work he had etched only thirty-eight plates of great Roman buildings compared with miserable Greek ones, but he had assembled 170,000 words on 212 huge folio pages of Latin and Italian text, which show his temper and direction, but were probably written by some friendly scholar whom he had rallied to defend the cause of Rome. Like other self-educated men, Piranesi probably overrated the value of pedantic authority.

The uproar was really over a matter of names, for Piranesi recognized that Rome had learned her art from Greek works like the Athenian painted vases and the Doric temples at Paestum—only he called these Etruscan. His eye told him the truth but his books misled him. To demonstrate the flimsy caprice of Greek architecture he cited—St. Mark's. Like the men of the Middle Ages, he did not distinguish Greek from Byzantine. But he was fighting a battle that was already lost, for just one year after he published his *Magnificence and Architecture of the Romans,* Stuart and Revett brought out the earliest accurate pictures of Greek buildings in the first volume of their *Antiquities of Athens.* These engravings settled the bickering quietly and for keeps.

Piranesi said that Rome showed her magnificence in "the sewers, the filling of the valleys, the walls of Rome, the aqueducts, the paved roads." He approached Roman buildings partly through his engineering experience from his uncle Matteo and partly by studying Roman engineering in Vitruvius. Business-like renaissance architects had measured the broken columns and entablatures in order to deduce rules of thumb to help them in designing new façades. They filled their books with diagrams of the five orders that became canonical by force of repetition. But Piranesi investigated for the sake of investigation and wanted, like a scientist, to drill into the core of the masonry and to dig under the foundations. "I have drawn these remains . . . . by means of sections and profiles, and have sometimes been able to show . . . how they were built through my many years of tireless close scrutiny, digging and study." He went at Rome's weedy lumps of ruin like an anatomist at a cadaver, stripping, sectioning, sawing until he had established the structure in all its layers and functions. Sometimes he removed accretions from columns imbedded in the slums of Rome until he laid them bare like bones in a loneliness of sand. His method is the method of autopsy and his books rank with the great books of anatomy, for he was the first, and remains the most dramatic dissector of ruin.

When he began his huge folios for the learned world, he also started to work for the lay public by etching his most famous works, the 135 big *Views of Rome.*

Rome had been supplying visitors with souvenir views since tiny rough woodcuts first appeared in the little pilgrim guidebooks of the 1490's. In the early 1520's Marcantonio Raimondi trained a group of engravers who produced a certain number of views. Then a succession of enterprising print publishers organized production into a trade so alert and adaptable that in the 1860's this Roman industry converted to the first profitable mass production of souvenir photographs. When Piranesi arrived he found that most of the views were being etched by a Sicilian called Giuseppe Vasi, who taught him to etch, and imposed his smooth straight style on Piranesi's early works. Piranesi kept this neat, ruled rendering when he etched Rome's modern buildings, but devised a more personal line to express the weedy crumbling of the ruins. After some months of instruction, Vasi is said to have remarked to Piranesi: "You are too much of a painter to make a good etcher." He was quite right, if he meant the etcher as the artisan who used to do the drudgery (now done through photography) of picture-making for everyday information. Book illustrations and prints on subjects of current interest could be produced rapidly and economically only by standardizing etching and engraving with such mechanical regularity that several draughtsmen could blend their collaboration into what looks like the work of one hand. Piranesi made himself great by breaking away from this commercially useful routine in order to explore imaginative vision. He attacked his big coppers the way a painter attacks a canvas, concentrating on the dramatic effect of light, air and depth. He is one of the few printmakers who never made a painting of any consequence and yet never let his mastery of print techniques distract him from the supremacy of imagination.

The Rome that struck Piranesi's imagination was not today's traffic jam that forces the population of a metropolis through the accommodations of a small town. His Rome surprised with contrasts. He passed from stinking black alleys to shady lanes and walled gardens. The marvellous town squares were already there—those opera sets in stone that architects have composed as adroitly as scene painters, to make every beholder feel that he is enjoying the spectacle from the royal box. But in Piranesi's day the wings and backstage of the scenery were board shanties and tumble-down huts.

Opposites jostled each other right and left. At the high portals of palaces the cowherds hallooed to their cows as they drove them to the grassy humps and hollows that had once been the Forum, and were then the cattle market. Here a washerwoman had strung laundry between imperial columns. There, inside the dimness of a crumbling temple, a blacksmith struck sparks on his anvil. And everywhere lean-tos rotted against walls built by Augustus and Domitian. Rome reminded Montaigne of the nests that swallows had plastered against the broken vaults of French churches wrecked by Huguenots.

The sweet air of the country was then forever blowing into Rome. Paths wandered among the grass; cypress and sycamore shaded damp mounds of ruin; shrubs rooted in the cracks of every old cornice and architrave, shimmering in the breeze and distilling their pungency in the sun. The Colosseum alone grew plants enough to catalogue in a special little botany book. What a jumble it was of old and new, of permanence and change, of palaces and shacks, of cesspools and cypress groves. No wonder that the city struck the Venetian's imagination and gave him something new to explore and draw every day for thirty-five years! Every chance to dig and probe and discover thrilled him like the eager labors of a lover.

The *Views of Rome* reveal his life progress as an artist. Though he dated only one of them—the Cascade of Tivoli of 1766 (fig. 103)—his sons' sale catalogue of 1792 dates all of them with some accuracy. He etched them from his first establishment in Rome until his death almost thirty-five years later, so that the series records the maturing of his hand and eye. In the early views a mild even light fuses buildings into a city landscape (figs. 25-28). Every window, every beggar and tree keeps its place in a harmony as tranquil and distinguished as Canaletto's. He etches the copper to a more or less even depth all over. Later he focuses on single buildings that loom up dark against the sky (figs. 44, 45). He makes some lines much broader and blacker than the rest by scratching them with a wide point and by returning them again and again to the acid, while protecting the lighter parts with coats of varnish. The final *Views* are often birds-eye panoramas that he had to construct from notes made on the ground or by clambering on walls. The ruins lie as black as though the Goths had burned them the night before. Hardly a living thing ventures onto the surrounding hillocks of cinders that lose themselves in volcanic gloom (fig. 127). Then the very last etchings of all recapture the wide unity of the first ones by dappling light and shade from cloudlets that fill the sky and by thickening the air between column and column (figs. 134-135).

Until Piranesi's time most professional viewmakers drew buildings in a simple, square-on delineation, like most portrait heads. They sometimes suggested depth by flanking the foreground with something dark on each side. Piranesi applied Ferdinando Bibiena's diagonal stage perspective to views of actual buildings (figs. 29, 30) and then proceeded to invent more different patterns for his compositions, more unexpected angles of sight than any other etcher before or since. Throughout his life he never stopped discovering fresh geometrical layouts, sometimes by sketching in mid-air from a rope sling.

Since Piranesi made his *Views of Rome* for a tourist public, he had to enliven them with figures. As time went on he became so interested in figures that he also put them in his publications for the learned world. He does not seem to have been formally taught to draw the figure, and often hired other artists to copy the nudes on antique reliefs. His first biographer, Bianconi, said that "instead of studying the nude or beautiful Greek statues, which are the only good models, he set himself to drawing the most gangrenous cripples and hunchbacks in all Rome. He loved to sketch twisted legs, broken arms, and sprung hips, and whenever he found one of these horrors by a church door, he thought he had discovered a new Apollo Belvedere or a Laocoon, and ran home to draw it." Even after allowing for the exaggeration of a wit, the story probably has some basis of fact, for Piranesi loved decay in all things to such an extent that when he introduced a detail of a building as though it were drawn on a small piece of paper, pinned onto the main picture, he made the pinned-on paper look like a dog-eared old scrap (fig. 74).

When he was in his later twenties he would seem to have studied the sixty-two little models for figure drawing that Salvator Rosa had etched about a century before. These once popular etchings show soldiers in fanciful "antique" armor acting with unsoldierly volatility—pointing to faraway disasters, striking attitudes with lances, whispering together, or plunging their desperate heads in both their hands. Piranesi did not copy these figures literally in his etchings but certainly took their mood of romantic unrestraint. As he pushed this mood into the hectic, it seems impossible that he did not do so through studying the paintings of Alessandro Magnasco. Magnasco died as an old man when Piranesi was twenty-nine, and though he painted in Genoa, Milan and Florence, his small canvases were probably well known in Rome. His special excitement animates Piranesi's groups of sickly brigands haggling over the contents of a tomb with a couple of convulsive connoisseurs.

Piranesi's figure drawing varied a great deal during his life. When he started to etch he was only up to indicating tiny lifeless dolls to give the scale (fig. 1). Then he must have made many action sketches in the street, for he filled his early views with fishwives and princes, beggars and prelates, wheelwrights and milords, which are the liveliest pictures of the trades and occupations of eighteenth-century Rome. As one looks at the gilt coaches and the beggars' crutches one cannot help thinking that since the days of Coriolanus, Rome has never had a buffer class between the rulers and the rabble, or any industry to absorb unemployment except the construction of huge unproductive buildings. The Caesars provided bread by building circuses, and set a pattern that every ruler of Rome has followed.

As Piranesi grew older his figures gradually took on more and more of an air of hectic destitution, until finally they have as little to distinguish their occupation as Michelangelo's nudes. The ruins become infested with tubercular wrecks, as though the race of Romans had decayed as utterly as their old buildings. The moth-like tatters of mankind who flutter up and down the crumbling great walls are too weak even to deface what their giant ancestors had erected. Such a vision might easily haunt an imaginative man in the Eternal City, where the dead began to outnumber the living so long ago that walls are now pigeonholed with tombs, every slab in a church floor rests on a boxed cadaver, and streets run over tunnels clogged with bones.

Piranesi's views expressed his romantic bitterness at not having been born an ancient Roman, his ambitions as an architect thwarted by poverty, and his dreams as a stage designer too vehement and angry for the frippery of his day. His pictures of Rome are the greatest ever made because he knew the city only by hearsay as a child and first saw it as a man. For the same reason Venetians were the first Italians to discover landscape painting because, as adults, rarely seen hills and trees struck them with the force of novelty. Piranesi's visions of fallen grandeur invaded the north of Europe like railroad posters that set people in a fever to pack their bags for Rome. But while his etchings startled the imagination, the actual ruins did not. Goethe complained that the Baths of Caracalla and Diocletian did not live up to Piranesi's views of them, and Flaxman told Farington that he had found the ruins of Rome "on a smaller scale, and less striking, than he had been accustomed to suppose them after having seen the prints of Piranesi." An eye that lacked Piranesi's stimulus of frustration could see only jumbles of masonry.

But the travellers who yawned at Rome could at least go home and build themselves more satisfactory ruins in their own gardens. Many of the fake ruins still survive in a state of real dilapidation, such as the ones at Schönbrunn, Bayreuth, or the colonnade at the Parc Monceau in the style of Piranesi's friend Hubert Robert. Robert himself anticipated the inevitable by painting the long gallery of the Louvre as a fallen vault and weedy walls, while the "sublime savageness" of Piranesi's views set Horace Walpole to imagining what St. James Palace would look like in 2,000 years. This was the first general effect on architecture of a man who had hoped to be another Palladio and originate his own style of building.

He never had an opportunity to construct anything extensive, but was commissioned to remodel some buildings when a fellow Venetian, Cardinal Carlo della Torre Rezzonico, became Pope Clement XIII in 1758. The new Pope asked Piranesi to do some work, now lost, on his villa at Castel Gandolfo, and to design an apse, never executed, for St. John Lateran. These projects must have pleased the Pope, for his nephew, Cardinal Giovanni Battista Rezzonico, a Grand Prior of the Knights of Malta, commissioned him to decorate his apartments in the Quirinal about 1766 (fig. 115), and to remodel the church of the Knights of Malta on the

17

Aventine (figs. 81-97). The last is Piranesi's only surviving work for the Rezzonicos. Originally the Knights had had a church dedicated to St. Basil in the Forum of Augustus. In 1568 they moved to the old church of Sta. Maria on the Aventine and built a priory beside it. A painting of the Madonna decorated the high altar until Piranesi replaced it with a statue of St. Basil. Thus the church is variously called Sta. Maria Aventina, Sta. Maria del Priorato or even San Basilio al Monte Aventino. Few tourists have entered the church, for it is almost always shut, but many have gone to the adjoining garden gate to peep at the dome of St. Peter's through the keyhole.

In 1764-1765 Piranesi strengthened the foundations and the vaults, redecorated the interior, added a new façade and designed a setting for the church. The interior is all frosty white plaster as clean of color as a classical statue (fig. 97). The decoration derives from Borromini's nave in St. John Lateran which Piranesi had studied thoroughly when he designed the apse to go with it (fig. 98). He had also studied the marvellous indirect illumination that Bernini devised for his statues, so that in Sta. Maria Aventina a hidden window floods the apse with light to make the altar stand out dark against the glow behind (fig. 93). The figure of St. Basil himself spreads out his arms like Bernini's St. Longinus. Since the altar figure appears to make a different gesture in Piranesi's early sketch (fig. 81), it may have been designed by Tommaso Righi who modeled all the stucco sculpture in the church. But the really original element in the altar is Piranesi's notion of stacking one rich Roman sarcophagus on top of another (fig. 92). The vault displays the symbols of the Knights of Malta: their patron St. John the Baptist, the shirt of humility worn in memory of the Baptist's clothing of camel's hair, and the galleys, rudder and shields for their glory in sea fighting (figs. 94, 95).

The church façade (fig. 86) originally rose above the present pediment to a high attic with three big urns, which was removed in 1850, a year after it had been damaged in the French bombardment of Rome. Thus the original façade was not squarish, but tall. Antique detail appears in new contexts, for the round window is made to look like the medallion in the middle of a sarcophagus, swords interrupt the pilasters, and the capitals are composed of castles and chimaeras. Piranesi also designed the approaches to the church. He decorated the wall of the priory garden with three tablets carved with pan pipes and tragic masks that suggest the lyric melancholy of the cypress avenue within and the bitter boxwood of the cemetery. The carvings stand out sharp edged like metal cut-outs against shadows incised with a burin. Piranesi had already etched ancient Roman reliefs of masks and shields and scabbards for modern artists to adapt. Here he showed how to dramatize the ancient motifs for modern effects.

One enters the garden through a charming building with a low pediment suggested by designs that Scamozzi had published two centuries before (fig. 96). These urns flaming against the sky and little obelisks topping the wall are bits of palaces on the Brenta and the Grand Canal brought to Rome by a Venetian architect for the pleasure of a Venetian cardinal. The little piazza is as wide and sunny as the villa walls that Guardi liked to draw when he crossed the lagoons to the mainland.

The Aventine buildings might have pleased a Venetian (the Rezzonico Pope soon knighted Piranesi), but the Romans disliked them. At least Bianconi, a year after Piranesi's death, says that "the work is over decorated, and even though the ornaments are taken from the antique, they jar on each other." They would have seemed less outlandish fifty years later, when Piranesi's designs had helped to launch the Empire style.

A year after he finished Sta. Maria Aventina he defended the adaptation of ancient detail to modern buildings by publishing a booklet called *Opinions on Architecture*. For one of the illustrations he loaded a façade with astounding agglomerations and topped it with a Latin motto: THEY DESPISE MY ORIGINALITY: I THEIR TIMIDITY.

Building and writing about architecture revived his early ambitions to publish projects. At forty-nine, just when the death of the Venetian pope ended his ten years of architectural practice, he published sixty-six plates of designs that were to affect decoration everywhere. He dedicated the book to Cardinal Rezzonico, who had commissioned his only important building, and he aimed the work at all Europe by writing a preface in Italian, French and English. The title states the program: *Divers Manners of Ornamenting Chimneys and all other Parts of Houses taken from the Egyptian, Tuscan, and Grecian Architecture.*

The book concludes with half a dozen plates of kinds of furniture that were mostly unknown to the Greeks and Romans, such as console tables, clocks and sedan chairs (fig. 115). Most of this furniture was designed for two of the Pope's nephews, Cardinal Giovanni Battista and Senator Rezzonico. The bulk of the book consists of designs for mantelpieces (figs. 111-113), which are the most conspicuous element of modern house architecture that did not exist in ancient times. "Among the numerous ruins of ancient buildings which I have seen and examined in Rome and throughout Latium and other parts of this state, I have not only not found one chimney in the manner of ours, but not even the smallest hint in favour of this opinion." The lack of ancient mantelpieces leaves the modern architect freer to invent. "What I pretend in my designs is to shew what an able architect may make of the ancient monuments by properly adapting them to our manners and customs.

With regard to chimneys, I cannot be of the opinion of those who would have no other ornament on them but such as are proper to a door or to the front of a portico. . . . If it were necessary for chimneys to resemble any thing, I should think they ought rather to be made in resemblance of a cup board or chest of drawers, than of a door or front of a portico. . . . I am rather inclined to think that chimneys form a particular class in architecture by themselves, which class has its own particular laws and properties."

Piranesi's designs put ancient details to revolutionary uses. The study of ancient monuments, of nature and of the ancient writers "have enabled me," he says, "to get out of the old monotonous track, and to present the public with something new in this branch. Some will perhaps accuse my works of extravagance, but . . . I shall be very easy by what names my works shall be characterized by such as think every thing extravagant which deviates from the old monotonous stile." Piranesi had repudiated Palladio for the spirit of Michaelangelo and Borromini, the spirit that reversed classical moldings and abolished architraves, imposed bold relief in front of low relief, broke columns and pediments, and upended obelisks, caryatids and pyramids in order to achieve dramatic shadow, active outline, and restlessness putting forth and pulling back in all directions. The real ancestors of Piranesi's mantels are not ancient Roman and Egyptian sculptures, but those declamatory Roman baroque tables and harpsichords and thrones that historians have unaccountably overlooked until their designers are now unknown.

All the grandeur that Piranesi would like to have expanded into palaces and basilicas had to be congested onto these mantelpieces. He packed so many ideas into his designs that they were to beget a whole new style fifty years later when history had prepared men's taste for them. Two events that were to lead to this change of taste occurred within a few months of the publication of the chimney book in 1769 —Wedgewood opened his new factory and named it Etruria after the vases that we now call Greek, and Napoleon was born.

Piranesi's designs travelled first to England, thanks to Robert Adam. Adam, who was eight years younger, had studied in Rome in 1754-1757, when Piranesi was in his thirties, both men drawing and measuring the ruins together. Adam urged Piranesi to investigate the huge complex of built-over ruins on the Campus Martius, and Piranesi dedicated the resulting book to him. In Piranesi's chimney book the first plate and the only simple design shows a mantelpiece that Adam ordered for Burghleigh House, built for Lord Exeter at Stamford in 1765. Adam got Piranesi to etch four plates of sections and details of Syon House to illustrate that masterpiece in his *Works in Architecture*. Piranesi wrote about Adam with more respect and affection than he showed for any other man, for both shared the dream of building for modern uses as gloriously as the Romans. Both men eagerly studied the exquisite bronze tripods, lamps and other household gear that were then being dug up around Pompeii. Since such beautiful things must have been designed by the finest antique artists, Piranesi and Adam did not think it beneath a modern artist to ennoble common things. They were the first two designers who held today's belief that an architect has not finished when he has planned rooms and a façade, but that he must go on to create the whole background for living—wall treatment, furniture, carpets and ornaments. Before their time—before the rise of modern personal styles—an architect did not have to supervise so minutely because he could count on getting a harmonious whole by merely sketching a general scheme for a corps of cabinetmakers, weavers and other artisans to work out freely together. The steadiness of the old royal patronage kept craftsmen living together and working in concert until their various products blended like the creation of one man. But as individuals began to accentuate their personal intuitions and discoveries, an architect had to draw every detail of a house in order to impose his own distinctive inventions. Piranesi designed many of his mantels with a matching chair and wall decoration to indicate the harmony of the whole room (figs. 112, 113).

The English took at once to Piranesi's imperial Roman style because they already felt the longings that were creating an empire even vaster than Rome's. England devined her future by looking backward into the mirror of classical antiquity. As if to educate herself for world rule, England led in studies of Greece and Rome with the work of Richard Bentley, who founded the modern science of classical philology in the early 1700's, Robert Wood's *Ruins of Palmyra,* 1753, Stuart and Revett's *Antiquities of Athens,* 1762, and Gibbon's *Decline and Fall of the Roman Empire,* whose first volume appeared in 1776. For such works Goethe saluted England as the leader in classical studies. Piranesi wrote to his sister a few months before his death that he would never return to Venice, but that if he had to choose a home it would be London because the English were the only people who really cared about the arts.

Piranesi was the first man since antiquity to revive Egyptian art for decoration. He tried this out with some lost wall paintings for the English Coffeehouse in the Piazza di Spagna at Rome. There he painted an Egyptian desert as crowded with buildings as Fischer von Erlach's, but his monuments are more accurate (fig. 110). The Italians probably did not enjoy gossiping and sipping coffee under the stare of sphinxes, bulls and Osirises, for when Piranesi etched two of these walls in his chimney book, he claimed that his Egyptian style was popular in England.

He developed Egyptian ornament with startling brutality in the mantelpieces in his chimney book. The style lay dormant until Napoleon's Egyptian campaign of 1799 suddenly sprinkled continental Europe with hieroglyphs and sphinxes, just as the discovery of Tutankhamen's tomb in 1922 put patchwork Egyptian figures on handbags and cocktail napkins. In America the contemporaries of Edgar Allen Poe adapted Egyptian pylons for hopeless doorways into prisons and cemeteries. The New York Tombs Prison got its name from the Egyptian façades designed in 1834.

Piranesi's imperial Roman style was made to order for Napoleon to glorify his Mediterranean conquests and to remind the world that former self-made emperors had become respectable with time. A world in the turmoil of provisional governments wanted to recall the stability of the Imperium Romanum, and a generation scattered by wars longed for the security of the Pax Romana. It is no wonder that people helped themselves to Piranesi's fasces and eagles to such an extent that some scholars would like to rename the Empire style the Piranesi style. Twenty years after his death his sons obeyed the pull of the times by taking all his copperplates to Paris, where they were printed perhaps even more than in Rome.

Piranesi's ideas reappear in Thomas Hope's *Household Furniture and Interior Decoration* of 1807, and Percier and Fontaine's *Recueil de Décorations Intérieures* of 1812, which named the interior decorator, created his profession and established his chilly good taste. The new rich of these shaken years were not so sure of their taste as the old nobility had been and so relied more on professional decorators. The Piranesi style held on until the 1840's when too much security turned people to borrowing trouble from the pageantry of an imaginary Middle Ages and other old unhappy far-off things.

The year before he published the chimney book, Piranesi started to etch over a hundred plates of *Vases, Candelabra, Urns, Sarcophagi, Lamps and Other Antique Ornaments,* which he worked on during his last ten years. He had become a dealer in Roman antiques which he bought or dug up at Hadrian's Villa and elsewhere, then repaired and sold. Cardinal Rezzonico bought some, but most of his customers were rich English travellers who passed through Rome with letters from Robert Adam and other English friends. When he got a good marble he advertised it in a smashing great etching dedicated to some likely purchaser (figs. 116-119). Reading the names on the dedications is like picking over the calling cards that probably littered a bowl in Piranesi's front hall. To some fifty odd Englishmen there are barely half a dozen from other nations, and only about three Italians. Fifteen years later the family's acquaintance had changed when Piranesi's son Francesco dedicated a series of etchings of statues mostly to Swedes, but also to Russians, Germans and a few Eng-lishmen. He had sold his father's antique marbles to the king of Sweden, and the French Revolution had made it hard for Englishmen to leave England.

In the spring of his last year Piranesi returned to his beginnings by going with a party of helpers to measure and draw the great Doric temples at Paestum. In early Christian times the silting up of the river had isolated that plain in such a malarial loneliness that the discovery of the temples, only fifty-odd miles south of Naples, in about 1750, surprised Europe as much as the excavations then beginning at Pom-peii. Piranesi spent part of the summer of 1776 at Paestum, which he already knew from former trips. He seems to have made a habit of sketching and measuring out-doors during the summers and then etching at home during the winters, just as Italian painters used to spend summers drawing from the nude and winters paint-ing from their drawings. On the spot, Piranesi sketched so hastily that his notations surprised Hubert Robert by their meagreness. Piranesi defended himself by saying: "The sketch is not on my paper, but in my head. It will show in my etching." (figs. 78, 79) Being away from the scene for his final etching left Piranesi free to forget unessentials, to design from remembered hints, to command shadows, and to create what Bianconi called "a beautiful infidelity." The same routine of work enabled the old Italian figure painters to simplify figures through reflection and under-standing.

At Paestum Piranesi measured the temples for plans and elevations that were never etched and are now lost. He also made drawings for twenty large views and etched seventeen of them. In these last etchings he attained the art that hides art, for he managed to dramatize the row of temples standing elephant-legged on the barren flats without resorting to schemes of stage design, and he somehow filled these pictures with his deepest fluidity of air (figs. 134, 135). The big country boys plodding after their cows were drawn by Piranesi's son Francesco, for Piranesi had not finished etching this last set of plates when he died on November 9, 1778, about five weeks after his fifty-eighth birthday. He met death with tools in his hands, too busy to see doctors, and working with his pencil and etching needle right into his last hours. After a time of burial in the church of the painters' guild, he lies today in Sta. Maria Aventina, surrounded by his only surviving architecture.

He spanned two worlds, like any really inventive man. While defending an outworn historical theory he helped to establish modern standards for archaeology. His original designs close the great Roman baroque tradition and start the first style of the next century. By looking back at antiquity he imposed on posterity the hallu-cination of a Rome that probably never was. This spectacular tragedian of decay

23

evoked the most obsessive vision ever dreamed of any city and cast a spell on man's imagination that architects have been trying to realize in stone all over the world. Rome's actual ruins are not impressive enough in themselves to have evoked a demand for such massive public buildings in London, New York, New Delhi and Leningrad. Their tall columns and emphatic façades are Piranesi's most conspicuous, though not his most enduring monument. Now that we no longer look at his etchings for archaeological information, we value them all the more for the splendor of their imagination.

Piranesi's epitaph was probably composed by Cardinal Rezzonico, whose last act of friendship was to give his architect burial in Santa Maria Aventina. The marble reads, in part, as follows:

CINERIBUS·ET·MEMORIAE

JOAN·BAPTISTAE·PIRANESI

DOMO·VENETIIS

SCALPTORIS·LINEARIS·AERE·CAELANDO

PLASTAE·SIGILLARI·ARCHITECTI

———————

LOCO·DATO

AB·JOAN·BAPT·REZZONICO

CARD·MAG·PRIOR·URBIS

ORD·HIEROSOL

PATRONO

INDULGENTISS

WHAT OTHERS HAVE SAID

MOST OF THE LETTER WRITERS, DIARISTS AND NOVELISTS OF the past interest us for the way in which they represent the fashions and forces of their age. The exceptional man of the past stands out because he differs from his age by discovering something new in the world around him or in the world within himself. He looks so intensely human that we hardly notice the by-gone fashions that he wears. Thus we think of minor Elizabethans, like Beaumont and Fletcher, as dandies in trunk-hose and doublets, whereas Shakespeare is a voice inside each one of us, speaking in words that fit our thought more aptly than our own speech. One test for a man's genius might be his ability to present facets enough for every man to find his own reflection somewhere. Piranesi was human to the point of violence. He evoked reactions from many critics that do not add up to a coherent picture of him, but do neatly characterize each critic.

It is odd that none of the tourists who visited Piranesi seems to have written a description of him. A year after his death his elegant biographer Bianconi said: "Piranesi was rather tall, dark skinned, with most lively eyes that never stayed still. His expression was pleasant, though earnest and meditative. He spoke more copiously than eloquently, struggling to be clear." He must have spoken with Venetian z's, for in the first state of the *Prisons* he spelled the French publisher Bouchard as Buzard (fig. 9.) In Italy a dialect indicates a man's birthplace, not his social standing, as it does in French or English.

The best portrait of Piranesi is Polanzani's etching (frontispiece) which shows him at thirty as a deep-chested, muscular man with a look that is solitary and formidable.

The earliest personal recollection of him may be in the introduction that Sir William Chambers added to his *Civil Architecture* in 1791. Chambers had left Rome when Piranesi, aged thirty-five, was living across the Corso from the French Academy. Chambers later built a casino for Piranesi's enemy, Lord Charlemont, so that he had a certain bias when he wrote: "A celebrated Italian Artist, whose taste and luxuriance of fancy were unusually great, and the effect of whose compositions, on paper, has seldom been equalled, knew little of construction or calculation, yet less of the contrivance of habitable structures, or the modes of carrying real works into

25

execution; though styling himself an architect. And when some pensioners of the French academy at Rome, in the Author's hearing, charged him with ignorance of plans, he composed a very complicated one, since published in his work, which sufficiently proves, that the charge was not altogether groundless." No such plan occurs in Piranesi's publications.

When Piranesi was forty-five Smollett found Rome still echoing with the quarrel that started with the publication of the *Magnificence and Architecture of the Romans* in 1761. Smollett wrote on February 20, 1765, that the most celebrated views of Rome "are the plates of Piranesi, who is not only an ingenious architect and engraver, but also a learned antiquarian, though he is apt to run riot in his conjectures, and with regard to the arts of antient Rome, has broached some doctrines, which he will find it very difficult to maintain."

On April 8, 1769, just after the publication of the chimney book, the painter James Barry wrote to Edmund Burke: "The dealers play into one another's hands and he (Piranesi) has heaped together a great profusion of marbles of one sort or another, which he would be glad to sell; but as nobody will be ever likely to mistake them for Greek workmanship, for a very obvious reason, the reviving and carrying into extremes his old prejudices against the Greeks will be still the more grateful, should it contribute to facilitate the selling of his collection. I sincerely regard him as one of the best engravers that has ever appeared in the world ... and he will go down to posterity with deserved reputation, in spite of his Egyptian or other whimsies, and his gusto of architecture flowing out of the same cloaca with Borromini's, and other hair-brained moderns; his avarice, which stimulates him to almost anything, would take ill what I have been saying, so that it were best you took no notice to any body of any of these remarks coming from me. I shall no longer have any fears when I get amongst my friends in England."

The criticism of his work outside Italy began quite early. One of the first accounts of his work was published ten years before his death in the second edition of William Gilpin's *Essay upon Prints*. Gilpin was one of those useful second-raters who have no personality of their own to color what they repeat from their intelligent friends. In his wavering account one can hear the battle of the *cognoscenti* in London. "The critics say, he has trusted too much to his eye, and that his proportions and perspective are often faulty. He seems to be a rapid genius; and we are told, the drawings, which he takes upon the spot, are as slight and rough as possible: the rest he makes out by memory and invention. From so voluminous an artist, indeed, we cannot expect much correctness: his works complete sell at least for fifty pounds. . . . His stroke is firm, free, and bold, beyond expression; and his

26

manner admirably calculated to produce a grand and rich effect. But the effects he produces are rarely seen, except in single objects. A defaced capital, a ruined wall, or broken fluting, he touches with amazing softness, and spirit. He expresses even the stains of weatherbeaten marble. . . . His stroke has much the appearance of etching; but I have been informed that it is chiefly engraved, and that he makes very great use of the dry needle. In a picturesque light Piranesi's faults are many. His horizon is often taken too high; and his forms ill-shapen. Of the distribution of light he has little knowledge. . . . His figures are bad: they are ill-drawn and the drapery hangs in tatters. It is unhappy too, that his prints are populous: his trees are in a paultry style; and his skies hard, and frittered."

In 1771 Horace Walpole prefaced the fourth volume of his *Anecdotes of Painting in England* with the first of the purple passages that Piranesi's etchings have inspired in English. Since English architects had become too dainty, Walpole urged them to "study the sublime dreams of Piranesi, who seems to have conceived visions of Rome beyond what it boasted even in the meridian of its splendour, savage as Salvator Rosa, fierce as Michael Angelo and exuberant as Rubens, he has imagined scenes that would startle geometry, and exhaust the Indies to realize. He piles palaces on bridges, and temples on palaces, and scales Heaven with mountains of edifices. Yet what taste in his boldness! What labour and thought both in his rashness and details!" Walpole could not have said more for the architect of the Castle of Otranto himself.

Italians considered his work more cooly. In his first biography, written a year after his death, Bianconi wrote that Piranesi was "the Rembrandt of antique ruins. . . . He seemed for the first time to reveal the Roman ruins to us from a distance. I say from a distance because on the spot we do not find that his picturesqueness and his warmth are always true. Though we delight in them they seem like a beautiful unfaithfulness." As a matter of fact Piranesi's archaeological renderings are often strictly accurate, but always manage to jostle the imagination more than another man's stage sets.

No contemporaries seem to have liked Piranesi as an architect. Barry lumped him with the "hair-brained" baroque, and Milizia, in 1787, dismissed him as "nefarious."

Piranesi's etchings slowly lost popularity after the 1820's, when the taste for classical antiquity began to share attention with the taste for the middle ages and the orient. By 1839 Paris must have lost interest since the publisher Firmin-Didot then sold all the copperplates to Rome. In 1831 the author of the *Life* in the *Library of the Fine Arts* wrote "his works are not sufficiently appreciated in England. Among us, his works do not bear the same prize as in Paris or Rome, where accordingly they are principally to be found. . . . His works, wonderful as they are in point of execution, are less to be admired for this than for the interest of the subjects he chose."

The great nineteenth-century output of catalogues of coins, shells, plants and prints more or less ignored Piranesi. He does not figure in the twenty-one volumes of Adam von Bartsch's *Peintre-Graveur* of 1803-1821, which is the first comprehensive and still indispensable listing of works of art, nor does he occur in De Vesme's more special *Peintre-Graveur Italien* in 1906. The first good catalogue of his books and sets of prints occurs in Albert Giesecke's monograph in 1911, and the first catalogue of the states of the *Views of Rome* is in A. M. Hind's book of 1922. This tardiness comes at least partly from the difficulty of listing prints that appeared in a confusion of overlapping publications. The only really good work on Piranesi has been done by Germans, Englishmen or Frenchmen, not by Italians. He has always been an artist for export.

In the Victorian world Piranesi went into a long eclipse. The thick index volume to Ruskin's complete works does not mention him nor does the index to Philip Gilbert Hamerton's *Etching and Etchers* of 1868. Any artist ignored by these legislators of taste could not be collected seriously in England or North America.

It is curious to see how shyly he began to reappear in the world's notice. In 1885 S. R. Koehler's book on *Etching* lumps the Piranesis, father and son, with "Canaletti" for a modest place in history by saying that all three "were architects and archaeologists who looked upon the subject of their plates with the eye of the historian. . . . Judged in the light of modern archaeological requirements, they have lost most of their value, although they will always remain interesting artistically."

In 1911 Frederick Wedmore's *Etchings* neatly situates Piranesi in the life of London by saying that his "plates are very large: hence unfit, often, for the folio or the hand. But framed, and hung together in a moderate-sized hall, they imply, albeit a little monotonously, that we find ourselves in the dwelling of a cultivated person of the older type."

Eight years later Pennell's *Etchers and Etching* echoes this dictum with a more violent bias: "He never, even in his *Carceri*—his best work—depends on the vital line. . . . Piranesi's prints make a good frieze, or line a stairway well, but they are not good to be set before students; he had not even the grandiose feeling; his perspective is as poor as his industry is great. Of course he is far better than the hacks of today, but he is not a great etcher by any means." To be considered worth demolishing is, after all, consideration of a kind.

Reginald Blomfield wrote a vehement appreciation in his *Architectural Drawing and Draughtsmen* in 1912. "I doubt if, among all his inventions of buildings, there is a single one that would be of real use to an architect, and his combinations of details were licentious in the last degree. . . . The draughtsmanship is superb, the design about as bad as it is possible to imagine. Piranesi's direct influence on design — that is, the motives that he may have provided for immediate conversion into detail — I believe to have been almost entirely for the bad. It resulted in that stodgy classic that prevailed in England in the early part of the last century, and appeared in quite another form in the pedantic and finicking designs of Percier and Fontaine. . . . On the other hand, no one ever possessed a keener sense of the dignity of architecture and of its poetry. The quality of genius, which raised him above other artists, was shown not only in his assured and astonishing technique, but in a certain imaginative outlook on architecture — in his conception of it as a great and even stupendous art, full of mystery, full of a profound beauty and poetry. . . . The art of Piranesi is not a manner to be learnt: it was the intensely personal expression of a wild and melancholy genius." It would be hard to weigh Piranesi more judiciously from the standpoint of a practising architect.

Finally in the 1940's Aldous Huxley fitted Piranesi into the framework of our own time. Speaking of the *Views of Rome* he amusingly comments on the figures: "Men and women are reduced to the stature of children: horses become as small as mastifs. Inside the basilicas the pious reach up to the holy water fonts and, even on tiptoe, can hardly wet their fingers. Peopled by dwarfs, the most modest of Baroque buildings assumes heroic proportions."

Huxley gives a new and really original twist to the dark riddle of the *Prisons*: "Considered from a purely formal point of view, *The Prisons* are remarkable as being the nearest eighteenth-century approach to a purely abstract art. . . . Piranesi uses architectural forms to produce a series of beautifully intricate designs, which resemble the abstractions of the Cubists in being composed of geometrical elements, but which have the advantage of combining pure geometry with enough subject matter, enough literature, to express, more forcibly than a mere pattern can do, the obscure and terrible states of spiritual confusion and *acedia*."

This apt comparison from *Themes and Variations* might have been suggested by the exhibition of *Timeless Aspects of Modern Art* in 1948 in which the Museum of Modern Art in New York hung one of the *Prisons* (fig. 21) beside a charcoal abstraction by Picasso. Both had the identical sharp-edged bleakness of the dispossessed. The *Prisons* fascinate because their abstract patterns are like clouds, or ink blots, or the cracks and stains on a wall, in which each man sees the projection of his deepest disturbances. They are Piranesi's only landscapes of the mind.

The succession of opinions shows how the quarrelsome archaeologist was gradually forgotten for the etchings that at first startled with rawness, then settled down as house furnishings and finally have become a part of the lens of every cultivated eye.

HINTS TO THE COLLECTOR

PIRANESI'S PRINTS RESEMBLE GOYA'S OR DAUMIER'S IN THAT ordinary impressions are too common for many people to think worth collecting, whereas the earliest proofs are too rare for anybody to find. In spite of this his work has continued to arouse more and more interest during the last thirty or forty years.

In Piranesi's *Letters of Justification* he estimated his small profits of about $375 per etching on the basis of 4,000 impressions from each copperplate. Such editions were gigantic for copperplates before the invention of electroplating with iron, for C. N. Cochin in 1745 complained that a careless printer had worn out one of his plates after printing only 100 impressions.

Piranesi made his copperplates rugged by etching in parallel lines spaced far apart and rarely crossed by hatching (fig. 68). The acid eroded the plate into deep troughs separated by stout metal walls. These troughs kept their edges to catch ink despite the abrasion of many printings. Crosshatching does not wear so well because the grid of intersecting parallels erodes little squarish mesas or plateaus of copper that present four edges to the wear of printing instead of two edges on the walls. Crosshatching is hard to bite into the metal as deeply as parallel lines because the acid tends to undercut each side of the squarish plateaus until they topple over and leave a wide flat depression that will not catch ink. Piranesi's manner of etching explains why his coppers could print so many quite brilliant impressions.

But even his durable coppers wore smooth under the production that he demanded and so forced him to rework his plates constantly. Rework tended to thicken shadows and to darken the whole effect, even in the skies. Thus Piranesi's late impressions are darker than the early ones, which is the contrary of most etchings and engravings. He had to rework his *Views of Rome,* the popular tourist souvenirs, more than his archaeological illustrations, so that nowadays it is harder to find the *Views* in good impressions.

There are various ways of telling early impressions of the *Views* from late ones. Early impressions are apt to be on thinner paper than the near cardboard of the later ones. In the first fifty-nine plates of the series early impressions (though not always the very earliest), have the publishers' address *Bouchard e Gravier* in the bottom margin. In 1800-1839 the *Views* were given one, and later two sets of Arabic numbers, usually in the upper right hand corner. Numbered impressions of the *Views* are usually poor.

Over one thousand of Piranesi's copperplates—practically all—were taken to Paris in 1798 and then brought back to Rome in 1839. Impressions after 1835 often bear the publishers' name below the picture in a blind stamp without ink, like a notary's seal. Thus a blind stamp of Firmin-Didot dates an impression 1835-39, one of the Calcografia Camerale 1839-70, the Regia Calcografia 1870 to the end of the Second World War, and the Calcografia Nazionale for entirely modern impressions. The *Views of Rome* with a blind stamp are worn out and flat, but impressions from other sets can still be good. A Piranesi collector must examine prints for the paper, the name of the editor, the numbering, but above all for the general clarity or muddiness, which he can learn to evaluate only after comparing many impressions.

The best guide to the collector is A. M. Hind's *Giovanni Battista Piranesi,* London, 1922, which has the fullest list of publications and the only catalogue of the states of the *Views of Rome.* The most detailed listing of all of the surviving copperplates is in the 1891 edition of the *Catalogo Generale di Rami incisi posseduti dalla Regia Calcografia di Roma.*

Really early impressions of the *Views of Rome* and the *Prisons* are hard to find. No progress proofs before the picture was finished seem to exist for any of his etchings. Proofs of the finished picture before the inscriptions were added rarely occur intact because Piranesi cut them up to sketch on the blank backs (fig. 99). This habit conveniently authenticates many drawings but has deprived the collector of the finest proofs. He also drew on the backs of letters (fig. 85) and of the manuscript of his prefaces.

He probably treated his drawings just as cavalierly as the proofs. Few seem to have survived out of the thousands that he must have made. Fifty-odd are now in the British Museum (of which nine were reproduced by the Vasari Society, vols. V-X) and about one hundred and twenty-five are in the Morgan Library in New York (of which fifteen were reproduced in Felice Staempfle's catalogue of the Morgan Library exhibition in 1949). Elsewhere Piranesi's drawings occur by ones and twos.

More of his drawings must lie among the large unsorted lots of Italian architectural renderings that exist in many collections. His drawings are often confused with the work of Valadier, Juvara, Mauro Tesi, Domenico Fossati and other artists. He himself drew so differently at various periods and for various purposes that his work is very hard to assemble. Until the Morgan Library lot was published in 1949 no one would have dared to attribute to him the remarkable Venetian rococo projects (figs. 2, 3). Yet it looks as though all of the Morgan Library group must have come out of Piranesi's possession, though a few of the drawings are obviously by other hands, as Miss Staempfle has pointed out in the catalogue. Even some of the drawings that are not by him must be connected with his work, such as the tame red chalk copies of Roman sculpture which are probably by Jean Barbault who helped him to draw antique figures.

When he was sketching on the spot for future etchings he drew firmly and simply (fig. 78). When he was making a project for a patron he cramped himself to render details since the drawing is in the nature of a contract (figs. 92, 94). But it is his first thoughts and free fancies that released all of his unmistakable energy and assurance (figs. 24, 81). Even in his most dashing indications he could suggest the solidity of a building almost as substantially as Michelangelo (fig. 85). The forthcoming work on his drawings by Hylton Thomas should help greatly to make his work better known.

LIST OF MAIN EVENTS
AND PUBLICATIONS

1720 born October 4 in Mojano or Mogliano near Mestre. Baptized November 8 in San Moisé, Venice. Father: Angelo Piranese, stonemason; mother: Laura Lucchesi. Godparents: Giovanni Vidman and Maddalena Facchineri.

About 1730-1740 said to have studied under his uncle, Matteo Lucchesi, engineer and architect; Scalfurotto, architect; Carlo Zucchi, engraver; Ferdinando Bibiena, stage designer; the brothers Valeriani, stage designers, and his brother, a Carthusian monk.

1740 to Rome as draughtsman on the staff of Marco Foscarini, ambassador to Pope Benedict XIV. Lives in Palazzo Venezia. Learns etching from Giuseppe Vasi and Felice Polanzani. A builder, Nicola Giobbe introduces him to the architects Vanvitelli and Salvi.

1743 publishes *Prima Parte di Architetture e Prospettive*, dedicated to Nicola Giobbe July 18. (Reprinted with additions as *Opere Varie di Architettura*, 1750.)

1744 writes from Venice, March 29, to Giovanni Bottari, librarian of Vatican, to announce his safe arrival and to thank him for favors received in Rome. Possibly works in Tiepolo's studio. *Invenzioni capric. di Carceri* (better known under title of second edition of about 1760-1761 as *Carceri d'Invenzione*) possibly etched about this time. Also *Groteschi*.

1745 from Venice to Rome as agent of Venetian printseller, Giuseppe Wagner. Settles in Rome on the Corso opposite the French Academy.

1748 Forty-seven little Roman views published in *Varie Vedute di Roma* with views by other artists. Reprinted in various guidebooks.

1748 publishes *Antichità Romane de' Tempi della Repubblica*, dedication dated July 20 (after 1765 reprinted as *Alcune Vedute di Archi Trionfali*). Has already begun to etch the *Vedute di Roma* which he continues until his death.

1752 marries Angela Pasquini. Starts *Monumenta Sepulcralia Antiqua* (later published as *Le Antichità Romane*).

About 1755 daughter Laura born, later helps her father as an etcher.

1756 publishes *Le Antichità Romane*, May 9.

1757 elected Honorary Member of Society of Antiquaries, London, February 24.

1757 circulates *Lettere di Giustificazione scritte a Milord Charlemont e a di lui Agenti di Roma.* Letters dated 25 Aug. 1756, Feb. and 31 May 1757.

1758-1759 son Francesco born. Later becomes his father's chief assistant.

1761 publishes *Della Magnificenza ed Architettura de' Romani.* Establishes his own publishing business in Palazzo Tomati Strada Felice (now via Sistina). (Formerly published through Bouchard, then Bouchard & Gravier.) Publishes *Le Rovine del Castello dell' Acqua Giulia.* Elected member of Accademia di San Luca, Rome, 2 Jan.

1762 publishes *Lapides Capitolini sive Fasti Consulares* and *Il Campo Marzio dell' antica Roma.* Clement XIII grants 1,500 scudi to finance publications in preparation (*Diario Ordinario,* 13 Mch. 1762).

1764 publishes *Antichità d' Albano, Descrizione e Disegno dell' Emissario del Lago Albano,* and *Antichità di Cora.*

1764-1765 remodels Santa Maria Aventina. (By 4 Dec. 1764 excavation in progress under church floor. July, 1765 foundations excavated and buttressed, and decoration is under way. Mon. 20 Oct. 1766 Clement XIII inspects completed work. Three inscriptions date rebuilding 1765. *Diario Ordinario* 15 Dec. '64, 20 July '65 and 25 Oct. '66.)

1765 publishes *Parere sul' Architettura.*

1766 Clement XIII rebuilds part of Quirinal to house papal officials. Probable date for decorating Cardinal Rezzonico's apartments.

1767 January 16, Clement XIII creates him Cavaliere degli Speroni d'Oro. He signs himself henceforth Cav. or Eques.

1768 starts *Vasi Candelabri Cippi Sarcophagi Tripodi Lucerne ed Ornamenti antichi* which he continues until his death.

1769 publishes *Diverse Maniere d' adornare i Cammini ed ogni altra Parte degli Edifizi.* (Published before April 8.)

1778 etches 17 of the 20 plates of *Différentes Vues de quelques Restes de trois grands Edifices qui subsistent encore dans le Milieu de l'ancienne Ville de Pesto.* Dies November 9.

1798 sons Francesco and Pietro take all the copperplates to Paris and start publishing there.

1804 Francesco publishes *Antiquités de la Grande Grèce,* etched by Francesco after his father's drawings.

1835-1839 works published by Firmin-Didot in Paris.

SELECTED BIBLIOGRAPHY

BIANCONI, GIOVANNI LODOVICO: *Elogio storico del Cavalier Giambattista Piranesi,* 1779.
   The first biography. Inaccurate but clever.

FOCILLON, HENRI: *Giovanni Battista Piranesi,* Paris, 1918.
   Excellent account of life in eighteenth-century Italy. Readable biography of Piranesi and of everyone whom he is known to have met. Useful and extensive check list of etchings.

GIESECKE, ALBERT: *Giovanni Battista Piranesi,* Leipzig, 1911.
   The first sound biography. Briefly states almost all that is known. Excellent catalogue of Piranesi's many and confusing publications.

GIESECKE, ALBERT: article in Thieme-Becker: *Allgemeines Lexikon der bildenden Künstler,* 1933, vol. 27, pp. 79-83.
   The most compact summary of events and dates.

HIND, ARTHUR M.: *Giovanni Battista Piranesi, a Critical Study with a List of his Published Works and Detailed Catalogues of the Prisons and the Views of Rome,* London, 1922.
   The most accessible and informative book in English.

KÖRTE, WERNER: *Giovanni Battista Piranesi als praktischer Architekt,* in Zeitschrift für Kunstgeschichte, neue Folge, vol. II, 1933, pp. 16-33, 9 illus.
   The only good discussion of Piranesi as an architect.

LEGRAND, J. G.: *Notice historique sur la vie et les oeuvres de G. B. Piranesi.* Manuscript 5968 in the Bibliothèque Nationale, Paris.
   Compiled with the aid of Piranesi's sons. Extensively quoted by Giesecke and Focillon.

Life of the Chevalier Giovanni Battista Piranesi (probably by James Kennedy) in The Library of the Fine Arts, London, vol. II, August, 1831, pp. 8-12.
   Contains a paraphrase of part of the sons' biography of their father.

(PIRANESI, FRANCESCO AND PIETRO): *Oeuvres des Chevaliers Jean Baptiste et François Piranesi,* Rome, 1792. Reprinted 1794.
   A sales catalogue that supplies dates for the *Views of Rome* and other prints.

SAMUEL, ARTHUR: *Piranesi,* London, 1910.
   An agreeably written and often perceptive account.

LIST OF ILLUSTRATIONS

(The references to Hind indicate etchings from *Le Vedute di Roma*. Thus Hind 3, I means the View of Rome catalogued as No. 3, in the first state, in Hind's *Giovanni Battista Piranesi*. The etchings reproduced are all from the Metropolitan Museum of Art, New York, except fig. 99.)

Frontispiece. Portrait of Piranesi, etched by Felice Polanzani, 1750.

1. Etching from *La Prima Parte di Architetture e Prospettive*, 1743.

2, 3, 6. Drawings in the Morgan Library. The orb and cross on fig. 6 connect this gondola with a king or his ambassador. Venice gave state receptions to Ferdinand III of Poland in 1740, and to Joseph II of Austria in 1769 and 1775. The gondola might also have been made for an ambassador's state entry.

4, 5. Etchings from the *Groteschi*.

7, 8. Etchings from *Antichità Romane de' Tempi della Repubblica*, 1748.

9-23. *Invenzioni Capric di Carceri,* the complete first issue of the etchings, numbered according to the second edition, about 1761, as *Carceri d'Invenzione*.

24. Pen drawing, collection of Janos Scholz, New York.

25. St. Peter's. Hind 3, I.

26. Piazza del Popolo, Hind 14, I.

27. Palazzo del Quirinale, Hind 15, I.

28. Pantheon, Hind 17, I.

29. St. Paul outside the Walls, Hind 6, IV.

30. Fontana di Acqua Paola, Hind 21, III.

31. Fontana di Trevi, Hind 19, IV.

32. Harbor and Quay, Hind 27, IV.

33. Palazzo Odescalchi, Hind 26, III.

34. Hadrian's Tomb from the Back, Hind 30, I.

35, 36, 38, 39, 43, 44. Etchings from *Le Antichità Romane*, 1756.

37. Ponte Salario, Hind 31, II.

40. Architectural drawing, Morgan Library, New York.

41. Drawing of figures, collection of Janos Scholz, New York.

42. Etching from *Il Campo Marzio,* 1762.

43, 44. Etchings from *Le Antichità Romane.*

45. Pyramid of Caius Cestius, Hind 36, I.

46. Hadrian's Tomb and St. Peter's, Hind 29, IV.

47. Basilica of Constantine, Hind 45, I.

48. Temple of Vespasian, Hind 44, IV.

49. Theatre of Marcellus, Hind 33, I.

50. Temple of Antoninus and Faustina, Hind 49, I.

51. Capitol and Santa Maria in Aracoeli, Hind 38, I.

52. Obelisk beside St. John Lateran, Hind 53, I.

53. Column of Marcus Aurelius, Hind 52, I.

54. Round Temple near Santa Maria in Cosmedin, Hind 47, II.

55. Arch of Titus, Hind 55, I or II.

56. Temple of Venus and Rome, Hind 50, I.

57. Arch of Constantine and the Colosseum, Hind 56, I.

58. Temple of the Sibyl at Tivoli, Hind 62, I.

59. Portico of Octavia, Hind 59, III.

60-65. Initials from *Della Magnificenza ed Architettura de' Romani,* 1761.

66. Etching from *Il Campo Marzio,* 1762.

67. Ponte Lucano and the Tomb of the Plautii, Hind 68, I.

68. Enlarged detail from St. Sebastian outside the Walls, Hind 13, II.

69. Detail from the so-called Villa of Maecenas at Tivoli, Hind 73.

70. Title page to *Raccolta di alcuni Disegni del Guercino,* 1764.

78. Drawing of the cistern at Castel Gandolfo, collection of Philip Hofer.

71-79, 82. Etchings from *Antichità d'Albano e di Castel Gandolfo,* and *Descrizione e Disegno dell' Emissario del Lago Albano,* 1764.

80. Temple of the Sibyl, Tivoli.

81. Pen sketch for the altar of Santa Maria Aventina, courtesy of Walter Schatzki.

83, 87, 89, 92, 94. Drawings for Santa Maria Aventina, Morgan Library, New York. The dove of the Holy Ghost in fig. 114 shows that this frame was designed for church use. The frame might have been made for the Priory of the Knights of Malta, since the dove is often associated with St. John the Baptist, the patron saint of the Knights, and the name saint of Cardinal Giovanni Battista Rezzonico, the Grand Prior.

84, 86, 88, 90, 91, 93, 95, 96, 97. Photographs of Santa Maria Aventina. 88 and 91 taken by John Bayley.

85. Pen sketch, probably for the façade of Santa Maria Aventina. The reverse is inscribed in a notarial hand, the lines being cut away at both ends: "di Nostro Signore per il canale di VS Illmo | (d) 'accordare a Gio Batista Piranesi, Oratore | ione della Gabella dovuta alla Dogana | carte papale, delle quali egli ha bisogno | cp (?) . . . alle antichità Romane . . . a | sieno g(ia) venute in Doga(na) | sieno cinque Le quali del . . ." 4⅝″ x 7″. This document is connected with Clement XIII's remission of customs duties on 200 bales of paper for printing *Le Antichità Romane,* 1756. This remission must have occurred some time after 1752 because the work is not called by its first, later rejected, name *Monumenta Sepulcralia Antiqua.* Courtesy of Walter Schatzki.

98. Pen drawing for the apse of St. John Lateran, Morgan Library, New York.

99. Proof before letters from *Antichità d'Albano* on back of Morgan Library drawing AB 65.

100. Baths of Caracalla, Hind 77, II.

101. Baths of Caracalla, Hind 76, I.

102. Le Sette Bassi, near Frascati, Hind 79, II.

103. Waterfall at Tivoli, Hind 75, III.

104. Hadrian's Villa, the Canopus, Hind 90, II.

105. Tomb of the Plautii, Hind 83, I.

106. Porch of the Pantheon, Hind 82, I.

107. Villa Albani, Hind 89, I.

108. Hadrian's Villa, the larger Baths, Hind 93, I.

109, 112, 114. Drawings probably connected with *Divers Manners of Ornamenting Chimneys,* 1769. The Morgan Library, New York.

110, 111, 113, 115. Etchings from *Divers Manners of Ornamenting Chimneys*, 1769.

116-119. Etchings from *Vasi Candelabri Cippi Sarcophagi Tripodi Lucerne ed Ornamenti antichi*, 1768-1778.

120. Arch of Titus and the Casino Farnese, Hind 98, II.

121. Forum of Nerva, Hind 95, I.

122. Piazza Navona, Hind 108, I.

123. The Forum, Hind 100, I.

124. Basilica of Constantine, Hind 114, I.

125. Temple of Saturn, Hind 109, I.

126. Branch of the Acqua Claudia, Hind 118, I.

127. Baths of Diocletian, the Frigidarium, Hind 115, I.

128. Isola Tiberina, Hind 121, I.

129. Porta Maggiore, Hind 119, I.

130. Baths of Trajan, Hind 127, II.

131. Colosseum, Hind 126, II.

132. Mouth of the Cloaca Maxima, Hind 125, I.

133. Santa Maria degli Angeli, Hind 129, II.

134, 135. Etchings from *Différentes vues . . . de l'ancienne Ville de Pesto* (1778-1779).

136. Arch at Benevento, Hind 135, II.

137. Etching from *Antiquités de la Grande Grèce,* Paris, 1804.

138. Tomb called La Canocchia (The Distaff), Hind 130, I.

Tempio antico inventato e disegnato alla maniera di quelli che si fabbricavano in onore della Dea Vesta; quindi vedesi in mezzo la grand'Ara, sopra della quale conservavasi dalle Vergini Vestali l'inestinguibile fuoco sacro. Tutta l'opera è Corintia ornata di statue e di bassi rilievi, e di altri ornamenti ancora. Il piano di questo Tempio è notabilmente elevato dal suolo: vedesi in mezzo la Cella rotonda, come lo è pure tutto il gran Vaso del Tempio stesso: quattro loggie portavano ad essa, e per altrettante scale vi si ascendeva. Le parieti del gran Tempio hanno due ordini, sopra il secondo s'incurva una vasta Cupola con isfondati, e rosoni, e termina in una grande apertura, dalla q.te dipende il lume alla Cella che le sta sotto.

Gio Batta Piranesi Arch.º inv. ed incise in Roma l'Anno 1743   15

1 PROJECT FOR A TEMPLE, PUBLISHED 1743

2 PEN DRAWING FOR A GONDOLA, DETAIL

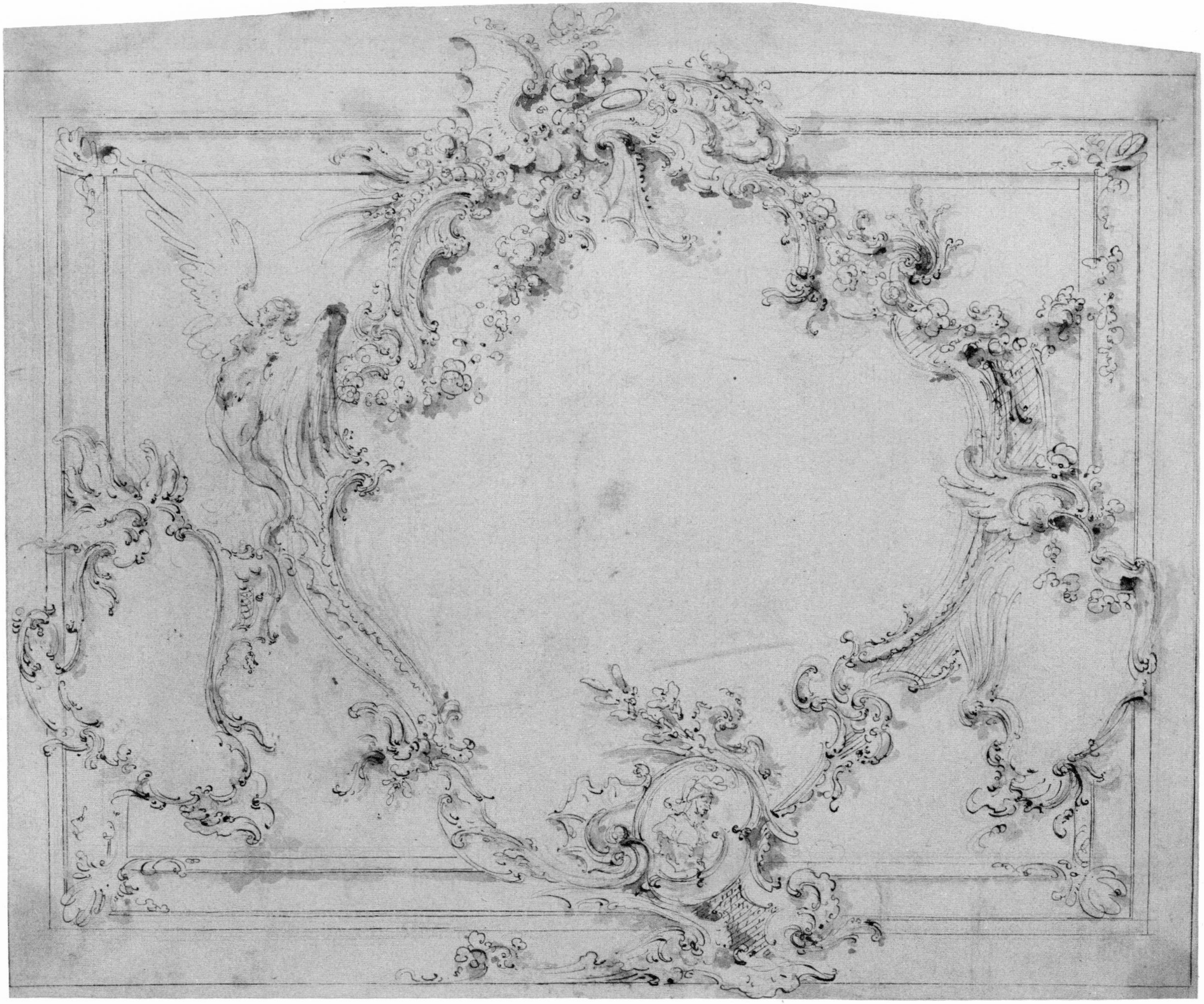

3 PEN DRAWING FOR A WALL DECORATION

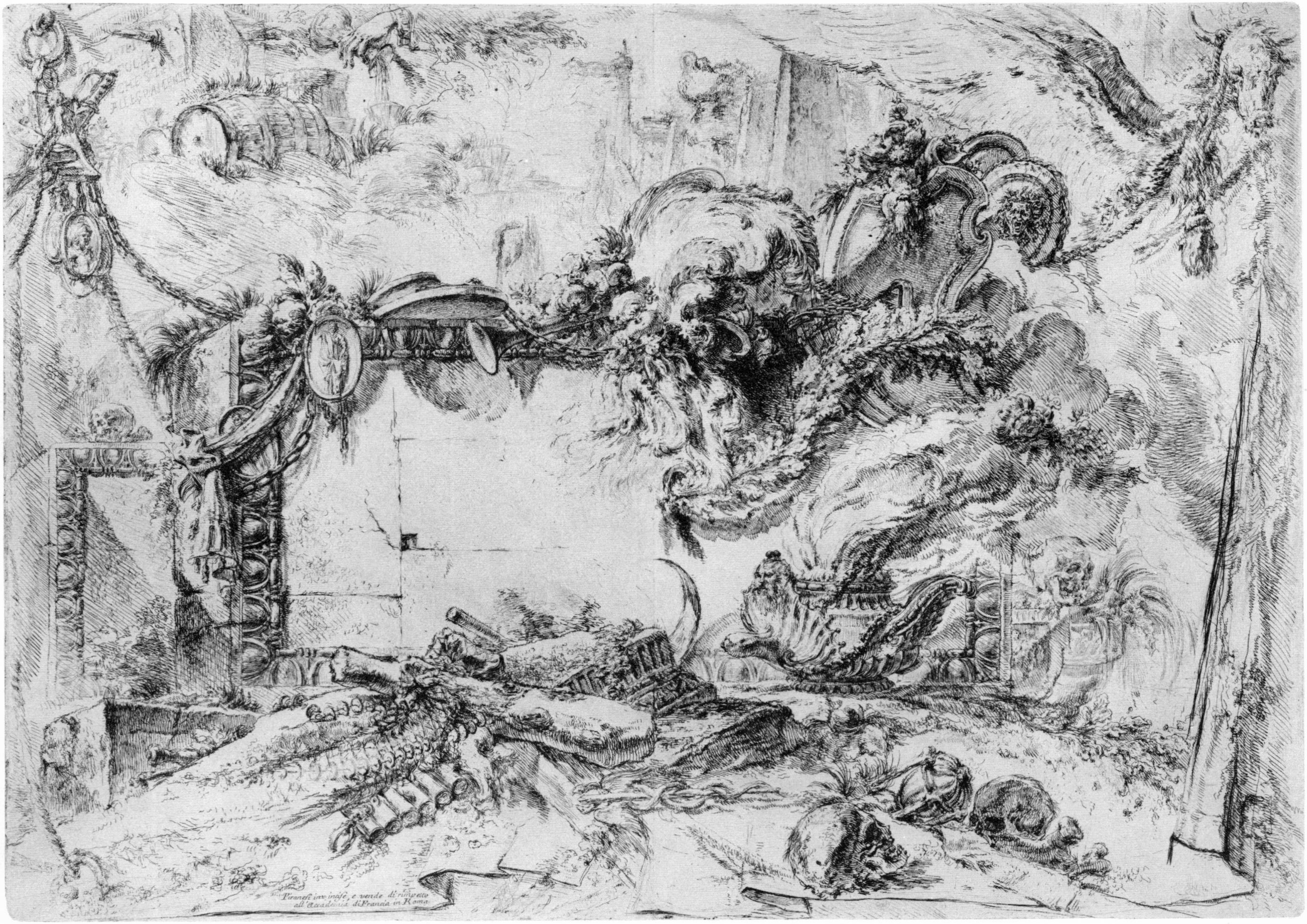

4 ETCHING FROM THE GROTESQUES

Engraved and printed in Rome
from the original ... à Brunel

5 ETCHING FROM THE GROTESQUES

6 WASH DRAWING FOR AN URN

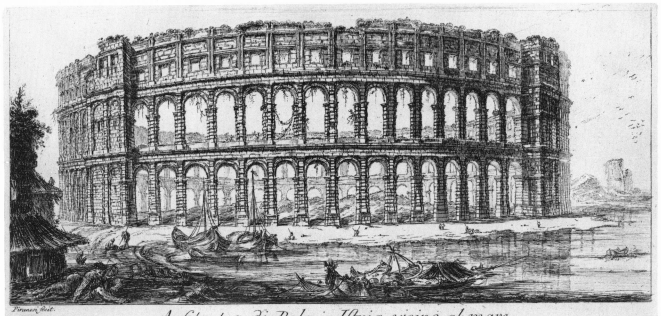

Anfiteatro di Pola in Istria vicino al mare.

Tav. 23

7 AMPHITHEATRE AT POLA

8 TRAJAN'S ARCH AT ANCONA, PUBLISHED 1748

INVENZIONI
CAPRIC DI CARCERI
ALL ACQVA FORTE
DATTE IN LVCE
GIOVANI
BVZARD IN
ROMA MERCAN
AL CORSO

9 PRISONS, PLATE 1, FIRST STATE

10 PRISONS, PLATE 3, FIRST STATE

11 PRISONS, PLATE 4, FIRST STATE

12 PRISONS, PLATE 6, FIRST STATE

13 PRISONS, PLATE 7, FIRST STATE

14 PRISONS, PLATE 7, SECOND STATE

15 PRISONS, PLATE 8, FIRST STATE

16 PRISONS, PLATE 9, FIRST STATE

17 PRISONS, PLATE 10, FIRST STATE

18 PRISONS, PLATE 11, FIRST STATE

20 PRISONS, PLATE 13, FIRST STATE

21 PRISONS, PLATE 14, FIRST STATE

22 PRISONS, PLATE 15, FIRST STATE

24 PEN SKETCH: ARCHITECTURAL FANTASY

1. *Piazza Pontificia fabricata da Sito V.*
2. *Loggia di Guilia d'architettura Di Bramante Lazzari, e*
dipinte Da Raffaelle d'Urbino.
3. *Guglia eretta da Sito V.*
4. *Vista tratta d'un prospetto d'entrata Orientale*

Franzei del. Scot.

Veduta della Basilica e Piazza di S. Pietro in Vaticano

25 ST. PETER'S WITH BERNINI'S COLONNADE, ABOUT 1748

Veduta della Piazza del Popolo

1. Chiesa di S. M. de Miracoli
2. Chiesa del' M. S. Monte Santo
3. Strada del Corso che conduce al Palazzo di Venezia
4. Strada che conduce a Piazza di Spagna
5. Strada che conduce al Porto di Ripetta
6. Guglia Egiziana inalzata da Sisto V

26 PIAZZA DEL POPOLO, ABOUT 1750

Veduta della Piazza di Monte Cavallo

1 Palazzo Pontificio   opere di Prassitele, e Fidia, Scultori Greci
2 Palazzo della Famiglia Pontificia   4 Quartiere di Soldati, e Scuderia Pontificia
3 Statue colossali rappresentanti li Cavalli, che dona il Bargello   5 Palazzo Rospigliosi

Ferenci fecit sculp

27 HORSE TAMERS AND QUIRINAL PALACE, ABOUT 1750

Veduta della Piazza della Rotonda

1 Pantheon fabbricato da Marco Agrippa oggi S. Maria ad Martyres   3 Lesteria
2 Fontana con Guardia Esistica architettura di Filippo Baratponi   4 Palazzo Crescenzi

Piranesi del.

28 PANTHEON. ABOUT 1751

Veduta della Basilica di S. Paolo fuor delle mura, eretta da Costantino Magno. 1. Laterali ruotici della Basilica che dimostrano l'opera esterna del detto Imperadore 2. Ornamenti, Musaici, e finestre, fatti ui dai successori Cesari e ristaurati da' Sommi Pontefici. 3. Portico con sette archi rifatto nell'anno 1725. dopo la rovina di altro consimile composto di nove. recorsa poco prima del risacimento. 4 Porta Santa. 5 Parte Settentrionale della Basilica verso Roma, e monti sotto de' quali è uno dagl'ingressi delle catacombe degli antichi Cristiani.

Piranesi F.

29 ST. PAUL OUTSIDE THE WALLS, ABOUT 1748

30 FONTANA DI ACQUA PAOLA, ABOUT 1751

Veduta della vasta Fontana di Trevi anticamente detta l'Acqua Vergine.
Architettura di Nicola Salvi.

Piranesi del. Scolp.

31 FONTANA DI TREVI, ABOUT 1751

1. Dogana grande. 2. Dogana del pesce. 3. Arsenale. 4. Granari dell'Annona. 5. Opizio Apostolico di S. Michele, ò Casa degl'Invalidi, di educazione nelle arti, e correzione de' Fanciulli, e di condanna delle Donne delinquenti. *6. Avanzi ad una delle pile dell'antico Ponte Sublicio, già di Legno, e rifatto porccia di pietra da Emilio, e ristorato da Cesari. 7. Avanzi delle stalina antiche. 8. Avanzi di muri de' tempi bassi falsamente supposti del detto Ponte Sublicio.*

Veduta del Porto di Ripa Grande

32 HARBOR AND QUAY OF ROME, ABOUT 1753

Veduta del Palazzo Odescalchi

1. *Palazzo Colonna.* 2. *Basilica de' SC VII Apostoli.* 3. *Convento de' PP. Minor. Conventuali.* 4. *Palazzo Muti.* 5. *Convento de' PP. Servili di S. Marcello.* 6. *Piazza de' SS Apostoli.*

33 PALAZZO ODESCALCHI, ABOUT 1753

VEDUTA del Mausoleo d'Elio Adriano, (ora chiamato Castello S.Angelo) ora chiamato Castello, S.Angelo' nella parte, opposta alla Facciata dinanzi al Castello. A Avanzo del Masso antico. B Coperonura moderna di mattoni sopra l'antico Masso. C Buche di Artiglieria, collocata nel Corridojo, che gira all'interno. D Loggia dinnanzibile, oppposta alla Facciata del Masoleo. E Carcere per le persone riguardevoli. F Archivio. G Molabino. H Angeli di metallo. I Baluardi fatti piantate dal Pontefice Alesandro VI. K Corridojo, fabbricato paterno per volta delle fossi: officia fatte coprire da Urbano VIII. Quelche Corridojo è fabbricate da cun numero d'Archi. e dal Palazzo Vaticano conduce sino dentro al Maiestlo. M Palcverina. N Cordonata, la quale porta, sopra l'Terrapleni, e sopra le Mura del principali Recinto del Castello. O Recinto di Mura, e Baluardi, che circonda il Maiestlo. P Armeria. Q Abitazione per gli Uffiziali e Soldati. R Altri Polverieri.

Preso l'autore a Strada Felice vicino alla Trinità de'monti A grade due e mezzo.

34 HADRIAN'S TOMB FROM THE BACK, ABOUT 1754

Tom. IV

X

B
E
C
D
A
D
E
F
G
F
L

Piranesi Architetto fece.

VEDUTA di un Ingresso alla Stanza superiore dentro al Masso sepolcrale d'Elio Adriano Imp.   A Soffitto formato in parte dai Cunei d'Intavertino, i quali compongono il grand'Arco nella Parete B : et in parte dai Crepi ordinarii; ovve da pietre Tiburtine, i quali sono posti sotto all'Arco stesso, come reintegro. B. Questo grand'Arco marcapiano rinforzato ne'laterali quanto si reflexiona al peso del Masso, peso altrettanto soffitto la Parete, abbenchè fa colmata dalla Fabbrica. C. Linea, la quale dimostra la Vista degli Arditi derivati nelli Tav. antecedenti.   D. Vistica, o sia Porzione de'sudd.' Cunei, la quale nella Soperie, che chi sfanno, fato Cornice il l'uno della due Parete, che di fanno, sato nulla volta di reddezza alla Fabbrica.   D. Vistica, o sia Porzione de'sudd.' Cunei, la quale nella Soperie, sono tanta magthea compesti, et importanti, fauregg. ogni altra imprefsione di ftraordinaria gravità, e solidezza: la quale si più dire, che non cede punto a quella dello rinomate Piramidi d'Efise. In cialcuna entra quivi a murare, e murare, Masfi con tanta magthea compesti, et importanti, fauregg. E. Brecce, le quali fervivano per addattavi le funi, et altave in opera i Cunei, come abbiamo dichiarato in più luoghi di questi Opera. F. Stanza, con Vista a tetto, ricoperta di moderna muratura. G. L'altro Ingresso, e Porta simile alla descritta.

35 UPPER CHAMBER IN HADRIAN'S TOMB, 1752-56

36 CONSTRUCTION OF THE TOMB OF CECILIA METELLA, 1752-56

Veduta del Ponte Salario

Tav.IV XXI

Piranesi Archit. del. ed inc.

Veduta del Ponte Ferrato dagl'Antiquarj detto Cestio. Dalla parte rivolta la corrente 1. Speroni moderni 2. Case, ed Orticelli nel Traflevere 3. Rovine di fabriche antiche 4. Catene, che tengano ferme le barche, su
le quali si macina il grano s. Pelo d'acqua in tempo d'Agosto

38 PONTE FERRATO, 1752-56

VEDUTA *del sotterraneo Fondamento del Mausoleo, che fu eretto da Elio* [...] *Adriano Imp.* In questa parte, la qual' è oppofta alla Facciata, gli Speroni fono tutti co- *ftruiti di groffi Travertini*. A *Parte di Riempitura, ovvero sia di* [...] Opera incerta a corsi, la quale vefte d'ogni intorno il Fondam. B Palizzate. C Parte del Mausoleo.

Piranesi Archit. dif. et inc.

39 FOUNDATIONS OF HADRIAN'S TOMB, 1752-56

40 PEN SKETCH FOR ARCHITECTURE

41 PEN SKETCH OF FIGURES

42 ANCIENT PART OF PONTE SANT' ANGELO, FULL SIZED DETAIL, PUBLISHED 1762

43 FULL SIZED DETAIL FROM THE ROMAN ANTIQUITIES, 1752-56

44 TOMB ON THE APPIAN WAY, 1752-56

Piramide di C. Cestio

45 PYRAMID OF CAIUS CESTIUS, ABOUT 1756

46 HADRIAN'S TOMB AND ST. PETER'S, ABOUT 1754

VEDUTA DEGLI AVANZI DEL TEMPIO DELLA PACE

47 BASILICA OF CONSTANTINE, ABOUT 1757

Veduta del Tempio di Giove Tonante

48 TEMPLE OF VESPASIAN, ABOUT 1756

Questo fu fabricato da Augusto, e dedicato a Marcello suo Nipote.   2. Capela de S. Maria in Campitelli.   Francesc. Arcangeli fec.

1. Palazzo Orsini restaurato da Baldassare da Siena Architetto.

TEATRO DI MARCELLO.

49 THEATRE OF MARCELLUS, ABOUT 1757

Piranesi Architetto fec. i. S. Lorenzo in Miranda di Speziali.

Veduta del Tempio di Antonino e Faustina in Campo Vaccino.

50 TEMPLE OF ANTONIUS AND FAUSTINA, ABOUT 1758

Veduta del Romano Campidoglio con Scalinata che va alla Chiesa d'Aracli
Architettura di Michelangelo Buonaroti

1. Abitazione del Senator Romano
2. Museo ove si conservano le statue Antiche
3. Palazzo de' Conservatori
4. Statua equestre di Marco Aurelio di metallo Corintio

5. Statue Colossali antiche di Castore e Polluce
6. Trofei di Mario
7. Colonna milliaria Roma
8. Liogallo di marmo Egizio

Piranesi Del. Sed.

51 CAPITOL AND SANTA MARIA IN ARACOELI, ABOUT 1757

Questo fu eretto da Sisto V. nella Piazza di S. Gio. Laterano.
1. Palazzo fabbricato da Sisto V. ora Conservatorio di Zitelle.   *OBELISCO EGIZIO*   2. Scala Santa.
3. Rovine di Acquedotti antichi.

Piranesi Architetto fec.

52 OBELISK BY ST JOHN LATERAN, ABOUT 1759

1. Palazzo Ghigi
2. Piazza Colonna

Colonna Antonina.

3. Strada del Corso

Piranesi fec.

53 COLUMN OF MARCUS AURELIUS, ABOUT 1758

Veduta del Tempio di Cibele a Piazza della Bocca della Verità.

54 ROUND TEMPLE NEAR SANTA MARIA IN COSMEDIN, ABOUT 1758

Veduta dell' Arco di Tito

55 ARCH OF TITUS, ABOUT 1760

Tempij del Sole e della Luna, o come altri, d'Iside e Serapi.
In Campo Vaccino negli Orti di S. Francesca Romana.

56 **TEMPLE OF VENUS AND ROME, ABOUT 1759**

1. Meta Sudante.
2. Radice del Palatino.
3. Vestigie delle Terme di Tito
4. Radice dell'Esquiline   Piranesi Del Sculp.

Veduta dell'Arco di Costantino, e dell'Anfiteatro Flavio detto il Colosseo

57 ARCH OF CONSTANTINE AND THE COLOSSEUM, ABOUT 1760

ALTRA VEDUTA DEL TEMPIO DELLA SIBILLA IN TIVOLI

58 TEMPLE OF THE SIBYL AT TIVOLI, ABOUT 1761

1. Due Frontespizj interiori del detto Portico. 2. Atrio *Veduta interna dell'Atrio del Portico di Ottavia.* reggevano. 3. Colonne inferiori all'Atrio
che sostiene il Frontespizio fatto per rachiuso da vittimo   muro con altri avanzi nelle cantine, le quali sostenevano i Tetti
Sicuro dopo l'incendio in luogo delle due Colonne che la   del Portico, ogni Escario.

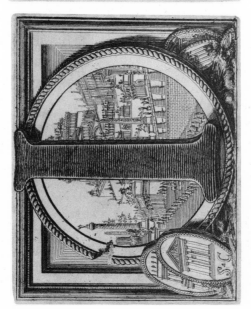

60-62 INITIAL LETTERS, PUBLISHED 1761

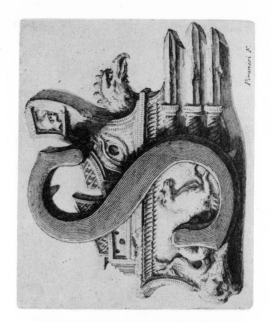

63-65 INITIAL LETTERS. PUBLISHED 1761

Tab. XXXVIII.

1. *Rudera viae Flaminiae.* 2. *Solum viae ab imbribus praeruptum.* 3. *Silices, et* 4. *Glarea, quibus via antiquitus muniebatur.* 5. *Iter novum.*
Vide indicem ruinar. num. 6, 7.

Piranesi F.

66 FLAMINIAN WAY, PUBLISHED IN 1762

Veduta del Ponte Lugano sul l'Aniene
nella via Tiburtina risarcito nei tempi bassi
A. Sepolcro della famiglia Plauzia

67 PONTE LUCANO AND TOMB OF THE PLAUTII, ABOUT 1763

68 ST. SEBASTIAN, DETAIL, TWICE NATURAL SIZE, ABOUT 1750

69 SO-CALLED VILLA OF MAECENAS AT TIVOLI, FULL SIZED DETAIL, ABOUT 1764

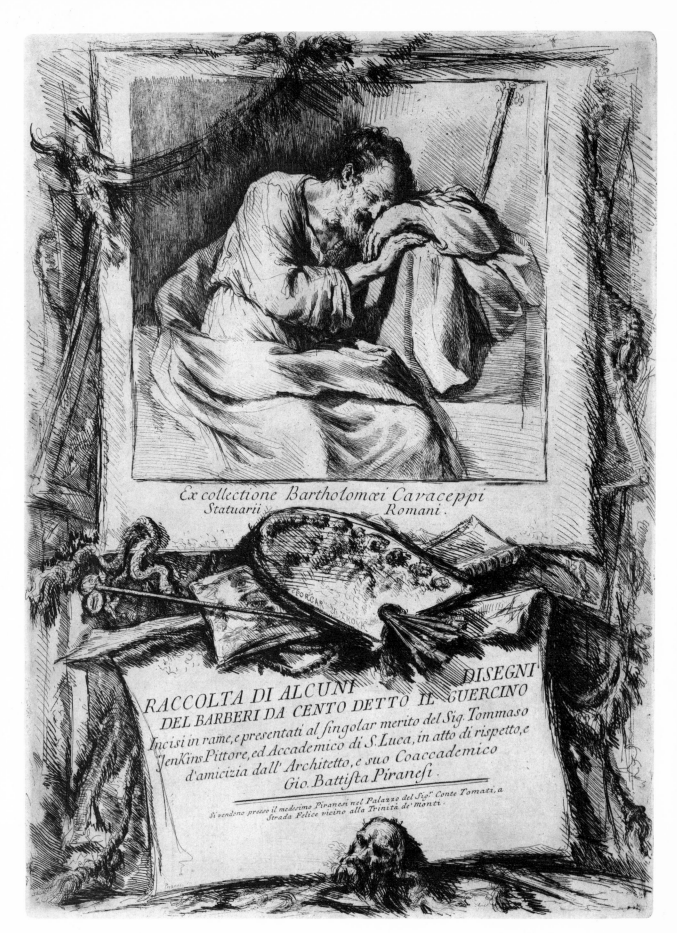

Ex collectione Bartholomæi Cavaceppi
Statuarii   Romani.

RACCOLTA DI ALCUNI   DISEGNI
DEL BARBERI DA CENTO DETTO IL GUERCINO
Incisi in rame, e presentati al singolar merito del Sig. Tommaso
Jenkins Pittore, ed Accademico di S. Luca, in atto di rispetto, e
d'amicizia dall' Architetto, e suo Coaccademico
Gio. Battista Piranesi.

Si vendono presso il medesimo Piranesi nel Palazzo del Sig.r Conte Tomati, a
Strada Felice vicino alla Trinità de' Monti.

70 TITLE PAGE, 1764

ANTICHITÀ·D'ALBANO
E·DI·CASTEL·GANDOLFO
DESCRITTE·ED·INCISE
DA
GIOVAMBATISTA
PIRANESI

71 TITLE PAGE, 1764

Prospetto del Lastricato e de' margini dell' antica via Appia, delineato così come si vede verso Roma poco più in quà della città d'Albano.

72 APPIAN WAY NEAR ALBANO, PUBLISHED 1764

Prospettiva della Scala della conserva d'acqua de' già detti alloggiamenti, accennata in pianta nella Tav. XIII. con la lett. G.

73 CISTERN AT ALBANO, PUBLISHED 1764

74 OUTLET OF LAKE ALBANO, PUBLISHED 1764

Tav. IV

1. *Rovine d'un antico Sepolcro, fatto a modo di vestibolo su la via Appia appresso la villa di Pompeo Magno, or fuori d'Albano, città situata in gran parte ov'era la stessa villa.* 2. *Porta Romana d'Albano, dalla parte occidentale.* 2. *Porta Romana d'Albano, dalla parte occidentale.* 4. *Dilatazione moderna della stessa via.* 5. *Villa dell' Eccma Casa Altieri.* 3. *Via Appia per venire a Roma, occupata in parte dai poderi e dalle ville che vi confinano.* 4. *Dilatazione moderna della stessa via.* 5. *Villa dell' Eccma Casa Altieri.*
Piranesi F.

75 APPIAN WAY AT ALBANO, PUBLISHED 1764

Tav. V
A
D
E
G
DIMOSTRAZIONI
DELL' EMISSARIO
DEL LAGO ALBANO
Piranesi F.

76 OUTLET OF LAKE ALBANO, PUBLISHED 1764

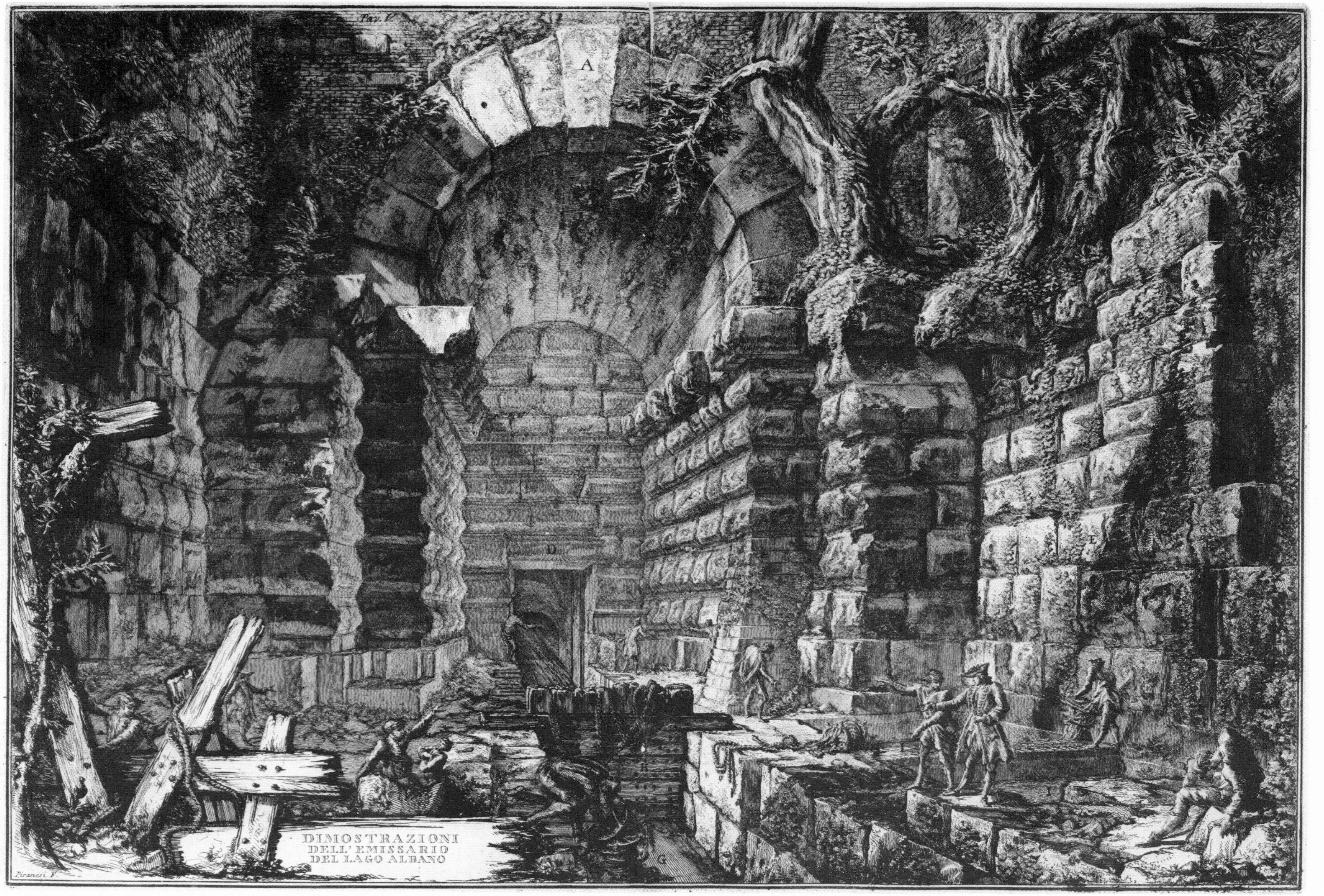

DIMOSTRAZIONI
DELL'EMISSARIO
DEL LAGO'ALBANO

77 OUTLET OF LAKE ALBANO, PUBLISHED 1764

78 RED CHALK DRAWING FOR CISTERN AT CASTEL GANDOLFO

Elevazione e prospetto d'un'altra piscina esistente nella vigna
de' P.P. della Compagnia di Gesu a Castel Gandolfo.

Piranesi

79 CISTERN AT CASTEL GANDOLFO, PUBLISHED 1764

Altra l'eduta del
tempio della Sibilla
in Tivoli
1 Sustruzioni dell' aja del
tempio dalla parte della
cascata del Teverone
2 Parte del Tempio sup-
posto d'Albunea

Piranesi F

80 TEMPLE OF THE SIBYL AT TIVOLI, ABOUT 1761

81 EARLY PEN SKETCH FOR THE ALTAR IN SANTA MARIA AVENTINA, ABOUT 1764

82 INITIAL LETTER, PUBLISHED 1764

83 PEN SKETCH

84 FAÇADE DETAIL OF SANTA MARIA AVENTINA, 1764-65

85 PEN SKETCH, PROBABLY FOR SANTA MARIA AVENTINA

86 FAÇADE OF SANTA MARIA AVENTINA, 1765

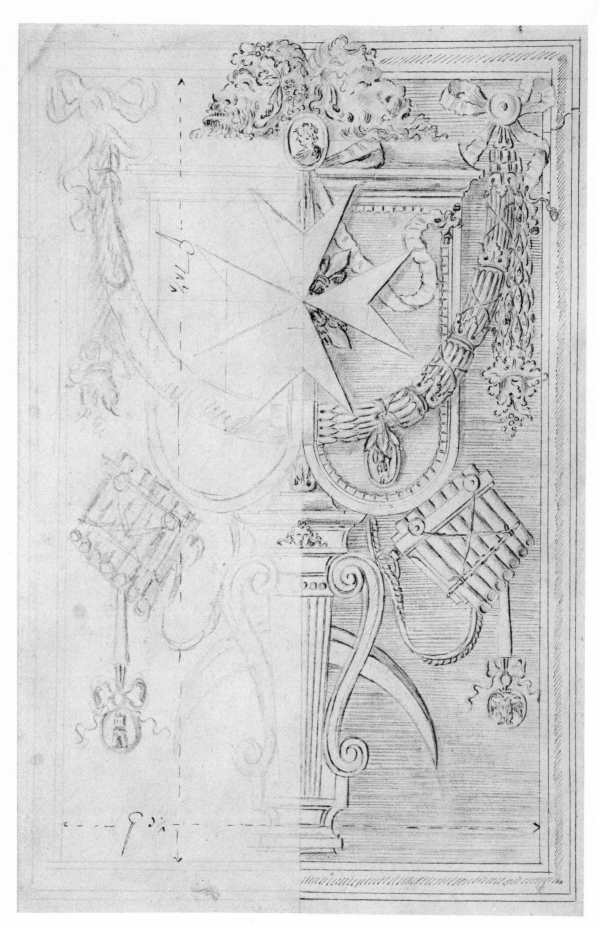

87 DRAWING FOR WALL TABLET ON THE RIGHT, SANTA MARIA AVENTINA, 1764

88 WALL TABLET ON THE LEFT, SANTA MARIA AVENTINA, 1765

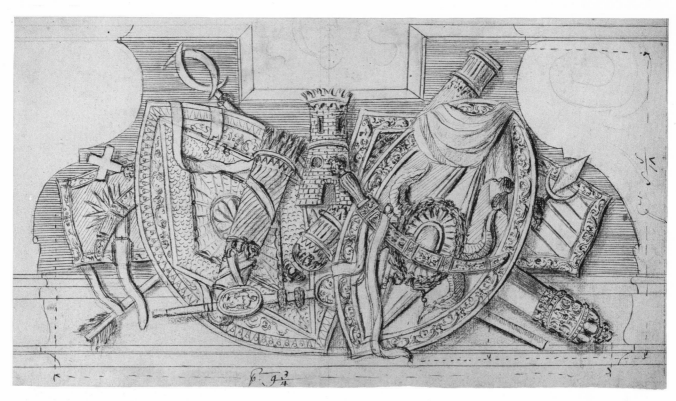

89 PEN SKETCH, 1764

90 DETAIL OF CENTRAL WALL TABLET, SANTA MARIA AVENTINA, 1765

91 CENTRAL WALL TABLET, SANTA MARIA AVENTINA, 1765

92 DRAWING FOR THE ALTAR, SANTA MARIA AVENTINA, 1764

93 ALTAR, SANTA MARIA AVENTINA, MODELED BY TOMMASO RIGHI, 1765

94 DRAWING FOR THE VAULT, SANTA MARIA AVENTINA, 1764

95 STUCCO VAULT MODELED BY TOMMASO RIGHI, SANTA MARIA AVENTINA, 1765

96 GARDEN ENTRANCE, SANTA MARIA AVENTINA, 1765

97 SANTA MARIA AVENTINA. 1765

98 PEN SKETCH FOR THE APSE OF ST. JOHN LATERAN, 1758-68

99 FULL SIZED DETAIL FROM THE ANTIQUITIES OF ALBANO, PUBLISHED IN 1764

100 BATHS OF CARACALLA, THE CENTRAL HALL, ABOUT 1765

Rovine delle Terme Antoniniane

101 BATHS OF CARACALLA, ABOUT 1765

102 VILLA CALLED THE SETTE BASSI NEAR FRASCATI, ABOUT 1766

103 WATERFALL AT TIVOLI. 1766

104 HADRIAN'S VILLA, THE CANOPUS, ABOUT 1769

105 TOMB OF THE PLAUTII, ABOUT 1765-69

Veduta interna del Pronao del Panteon

Sostenuto da sedici colonne di granito syn' una di fior, di un sol pezzo grosse di diametro palmi 6.6 alte palmi 63. 8. A Pilastri, architravi, e reste della porta composti di gran macigni di marmo greco. B Lacunari, di legname, anticamente di bronzo tolti via da Urbano VIII, e fatti rifondere per formare la confezione di S. Pietro in Vaticano. C Nicchioni dove erano collocate le statue di Augusto e di Agrippa, quali erano incrostate di marmegiata. D Pareti da dove furono levate le lastre di granito al tempo di Benedetto XIV. l'anno 1757. per adornare il Museo Sagro nel Vaticano. E Memorie di Urbano VIII. F Porta di bronzo trasportata da altro edifizio antico, ed in parte nuovamente ristaurata nel detto 'anno 1757. G Interno del Tempio.

Cavalier Piranesi F.

106 PORCH OF THE PANTHEON, ABOUT 1769

107 VILLA ALBANI, ABOUT 1769

108 HADRIAN'S VILLA, THE LARGER BATHS, ABOUT 1770

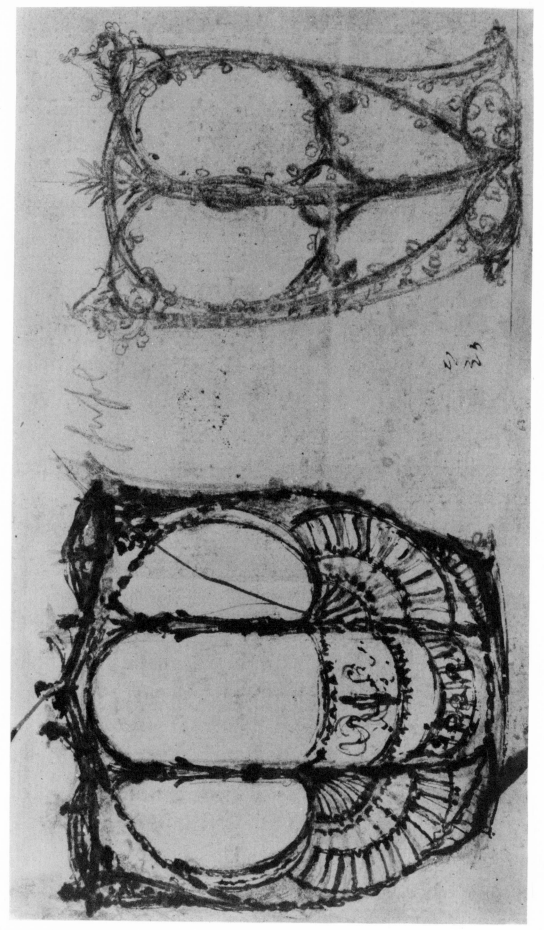

109 SKETCH FOR AN EGYPTIAN COACH AND A SEDAN CHAIR, ABOUT 1768

Altro spaccato per longo della stessa bottega, ove si vedono fra le aperture del vestibolo le immense piramidi, ed altri
edifizj sepolcrali ne' deserti dell' Egitto.

Disegno ed invenzione del Cavalier Piranesi.

Cav. Piranesi F.

45

110 WALL DECORATION FOR THE ENGLISH COFFEEHOUSE, PUBLISHED 1769

111 ETCHING FOR AN EGYPTIAN MANTELPIECE, PUBLISHED IN 1769

112 PEN DRAWING FOR A MANTELPIECE, ABOUT 1768

Cavalier Piranesi inv. e inc.

113 ETCHING FOR A MANTELPIECE, PUBLISHED 1769

114 PEN DRAWING FOR A FRAME

Questo tavolino ed alcuni altri ornamenti che sono sparsi in quest'opera, si vedono nell' appartamento di Sua Eccza Monsigr. D. Gio: Batta Rezzonico Nipote e Maggiorduomo di N. S. PP. Clemente XIII.

Cavalier Piranesi inv. e inc.

115 FURNITURE DESIGNED FOR CARDINAL REZZONICO, PUBLISHED 1769

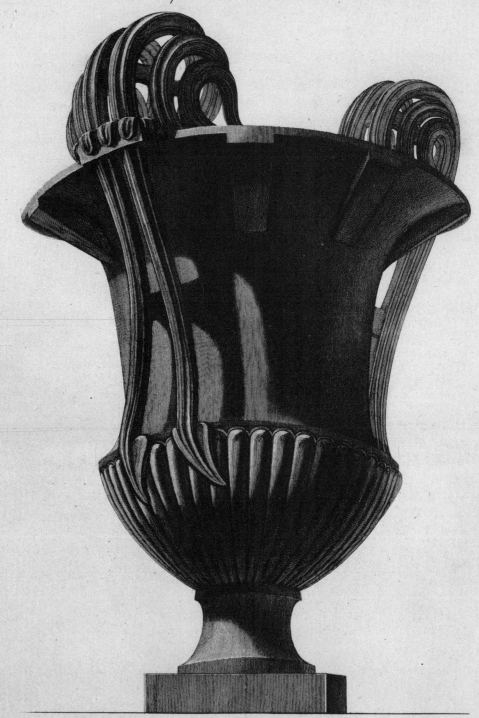

Al Signor Cavalier Giovanni Cuthbert amatore delle belle arti.
In atto d'Ossequio il Cavalier Gio. Batta Piranesi D.D.D.

Vaso antico di marmo di gran mole, che si rende particolare per
l'eleganza de suoi manichi, quali formano tutto il principale ornamento
di esso, e si vede nel cortile del Monistero di S. Cecilia in Trastevere.

Cavalier Piranesi del e inc.

116 ANTIQUE MARBLE URN, ABOUT 1771

Veduta in prospettiva di un candelabro antico
di marmo, di gran mole. Si vede nel Museo del
Cavalier Piranesi. Si rende pregievole per l'e-
legante varietà, e idea dell'intagli con finez-
za di gusto scolpiti, e sue sculture con leggia-
dra distribuzione à grottesco disposte, di maniera che non ingombrano essi l'idea generale
del suo tutto. Fù ritrovato frà le altre antichità
nello scavo fatto l'anno 1769. nel sito detto Pan-
tanello due miglia lontano da Tivoli posseduta
dalla famiglia de Sig.ri Lolli, ed era anticamente detto sito un lago appartenente alle delizie
della Villa Adriana.

fù diseccato con grande spesa dal Sig.r
Gavino Hamilton Cav.re e Pittore Inglese,
come si trova in oggi, nel sudetto anno, e
si vede dalli scoli delle acque di quelle col-
line, che lo circondano, uscire per quelli es-
purgato condotto antico, fatto ripulire dal
sudetto Signore Inglese, per fare detto scavo, dove si ritrovò gran quantità di bel-
lissime sculture, parte che adornavano
lo stesso lago, e parte à bella posta por-
tate ne tempi posteriori per riempire il
lago medesimo. Il di cui sito, e sua cir-
conferenza appena in oggi si riconosce.

Al suo Carissimo Amico il Sig.r Giacomo Byres Architetto Scozzese
Il Cavalier Piranesi.

Cav.r Piranesi F.

117 CANDELABRA FROM HADRIAN'S VILLA, ABOUT 1774

Altra Veduta di fianco del Tro-
feo, dimostrato di facciata nella
Tavola precedente. Lo Scultore
ha nobilm. espresso questo Sogg.to,
disponendo ogni sua parte con ma-
està, ed eleganza. L'esecuzione è de-
gna d'essere ammessa frà le Serie
delle Opere eseguite da valenti
Artisti in tal genere. La Coraz-
za è mancante del suo Elmo Greco.
Noi abbiamo qui in disegno perciò
supplito una tal mancanza dagli
indizj rimasti nelle sue ant.che Rotture.

L'abbiamo supplito di forma Greca per
adattarsi all'altro Elmo, che si vede po-
sato frà quelle spoglie, che viene calcato
dalla fig.a della Vittoria. Il Supplem.to del-
l'Elmo sudd.to qui disegnato è stato ideato
a nostro capriccio, seguendo però le tracce
già dette, variandolo dall'anteced.te Fig.a per
non assoggettare quest'aggiunta ad una
sola Invenzione, che è stata da noi ideata
ma disegnarla, supponendola in due diverse maniere, acciocche ognuno giudichi qual
delli due possa essere il più confacente sup-
plem.to adattato alla stessa erudita Invenzione.

A Sua Eccellenza il Sig. Principe D. Abondio Rezzonico
Senatore di Roma Amatore delle belle arti
In atto di Ossequio il Cavalier Gio. Batta Piranesi D.D.D.

Cav. Piranesi F.

118 ANTIQUE MARBLE IN VATICAN MUSEUM, ABOUT 1776

Veduta dell'altra parte del Sepolcro di URBANUS AVG. N. VERN. ET FABIA SUCCESSA Liberti d'uno degli Augusti. Questo Sepolcro antico di Marmo di gran mole era certam. uno de' principali Ornam. nella Stanza, ove fu trovato. I suoi intagli che si veggono in questo Sepolcro, sono allusivi alle Ceremonie usate dalli Romani ne i loro Funerale. Egli è adornato senza confusione per mezzo d'essi, i quali sono stati eseguiti da un felice, e bon inteso Scalpello. Lo Scultore si è sforzato d'assomigliar l'arte alla natura, la quale è stata immitata, come si vede nella gene-ral forma di essi intagli. La parte superiore è adornata con un Vaso a Cornucopia d'egual forma di quelli, che si chiamavano Uri, de' quali i Romani se ne servivano nelle Mense, e ne' Libami. Esso comincia con una Testa di Cinghiale, d'onde nascono Frondi, Rose, Steli, i quali vanno serpeggiando nel corpo del Vaso con altri ornam. Nel Basamento evvi l'Urna, nella quale erano riposte le Ceneri delle due suddette Persone.

Questo Sepolcro è stato ritrovato sulla Via Appia vicino a Capo di Bove nella Vigna Cenci, e si conserva nel Museo dell'Autore.

Cav. Piranesi F.

Alla Sig. Marchesa Margarita Sparapani Gentili Boccapadule Amatrice delle belle Arti.

In atto di Ossequio il Cavalier Gio. Batta Piranesi D. D. D.

119 ANTIQUE MARBLE NOW IN STOCKHOLM, ABOUT 1776

120 ARCH OF TITUS AND THE FARNESE CASINO, ABOUT 1771

VEDVTA DEL FRAMENTI
DEL FORO DI NERVA.

121 FORUM OF NERVA, ABOUT 1770

Veduta di Piazza Navona
sopra le rovine del Circo
Agonale

122 PIAZZA NAVONA WITH SANT' AGNESE ON THE LEFT, ABOUT 1773

Veduta di Campo Vaccino

123 THE FORUM, ABOUT 1772

124 BASILICA OF CONSTANTINE, ABOUT 1774

125 TEMPLE OF SATURN, ABOUT 1774

126 BRANCH OF THE ACQUA CLAUDIA, ABOUT 1775

Veduta degli avanzi superiori delle Terme di Diocleziano detto Santa Maria degli Angeli.

Cavalier Piranesi F.

127 BATHS OF DIOCLETIAN, ABOUT 1774

128 ISOLA TIBERINA, ABOUT 1775

129 PORTA MAGGIORE, ABOUT 1775

VEDUTA *Degli Avanzi delle Fabbriche del Secondo ... delle Terme ...*
A. *Primo Piano.* B. *Avanzi del Teatro. ...*

130 BATHS OF TRAJAN, ABOUT 1776

131 COLOSSEUM, ABOUT 1776

VEDUTA delle antiche Sostruzioni, fatte da Tarquinio Superbo dette al Bel Lido, come altri volevo d' Ercole il quale era situato nell' antico Foro Boario.   B Tempio di Cibele, o come altri credo da Marco Agrippa a tempi di   C Avanzi delle antiche
Acquedotti in creazione, ch' Egli fece ripurgare tutte le cloache, fino al Tevere.   A Sbocco della Cloaca Massima al medesimo Fiume.   D Monistero e Chiesa di S. Alessio.   E Priorato della Nuova Religione di Malta.   Salini.
Cav. Piranesi F.

132 OUTLET OF THE CLOACA MAXIMA, ABOUT 1776

133 SANTA MARIA DEGLI ANGELI, FORMERLY THE BATHS OF DIOCLETIAN, ABOUT 1776

134 PAESTUM, 1778

135 PAESTUM, 1778

Vüe des restes de l'arrière du Temple du Primaire du Temple de Neptune désignés dans les deux planches précédentes. A Pilastre rendu d'une proportion plus élégante que celui B. L'on remue à côte d'eux les restes C. des Murs internes de la Celle. D Restes de deux rangs de Colonnes qui étoient situées dans la Celle du Temple.

Cav. Piranesi F.

136 ARCH AT BENEVENTO, ABOUT 1778

137 POMPEII, ETCHED BY FRANCESCO PIRANESI AFTER HIS FATHER, PUBLISHED 1804

Avanzi è un antico Sepolcro, oggi detto la Conocchia, che si vede poco lungi dalla Porta di Capua per andar a Napoli. Questo Sepolcro non si sa a qual Famiglia abbia potuto appartenere, stante che gli è stata levata la sua antica Iscrizione. Cav. Piranesi F.

138 TOMB CALLED LA CANOCCHIA ON THE APPIAN WAY NEAR CAPUA, ABOUT 1776